THE *Psychic* YELLOW BRICK ROAD

THE *Psychic* YELLOW BRICK ROAD

How to Find the Real Wizards and Avoid the Flying Monkeys

CORBIE MITLEID

Contact information at https://corbiemitleid.com/contact

COVER DESIGN: Heidi Sutherlin
EDITOR: Berni Xiong
BOOK DESIGN: The Troy Book Makers

ISBN: 978-1-61468-423-7

DEDICATION

*Dedicated to every client I have ever had:
from seekers to skeptics, and everyone in
between. Without your participation over the
past decades, this book would not exist.*

*To those just starting on the road of
Enlightenment: you are very welcome
indeed! There is always room for more
folks at the Party of Life.*

But most of all...

To the late great Allie Cheslick,
"Chatty Cathy of the Dead" and the best
medium I've ever known. You predicted
this book, dear friend—and here it is.

REVIEWS

"For those looking for a trusty guide into the Psychic Arena Universe, a really good place to start is *The Psychic Yellow Brick Road*. Corbie's work is always first rate—not just as an author, but also as a trusted and very talented psychic adviser. She is, for sure, the real thing and this book is fun to read, gives LOTS of the Inside Scoop from someone who's 'been there, done that,' and is a handy road map for people at all levels of experience. An Ivy League-educated woman (literally) with highly developed skills in so many things, Corbie has my 'Haunted Housekeeping Seal of Approval.'"

— ANDREW BREWER
"The Rock n Roll Psychic," listed in multiple publications as
"One of the Top 50 Psychics in the World"

"With so many pretenders and Trained-In-A-Weekend 'Experts' in the psychic field, it can be difficult to know who is the real deal. Following the practical and sage advice in *The Psychic Yellow Brick Road* eases the mind and heart, so it no longer becomes a trial-and-error experiment in 'Is this the right one?' When you can determine the proper questions to ask and how to follow through on what you learn, you will unerringly find the right person to walk with you on Life's Learning Road."

— CHRISTINE ALEXANDRIA
Angel Intuitive and award-winning inspirational author
(*Askfirmations, Angel Chatter,* and
Have You Ever Wondered About Angels?)

"While psychic development books are plentiful, it's rare to find a volume specifically dedicated to the person who wants to work with a psychic, rather than become one themselves. *The Psychic Yellow Brick Road* is smart, sensible, and doesn't fly over the reader's head with jargon and hyperbole. Instead, it clearly explains why working with an intuitive counselor is a useful method for identifying challenges and gives you new tools to surmount them. We've needed a "field guide" like this for a long time!"

— STACI WELLS
Psychic Medium, Medical Intuitive, Numerologist, and Principal Soul Plan Psychic in *Your Soul's Plan*, and *Your Soul's Gift*, specializing in Karma and Pre-Birth Planning Readings

"Corbie Mitleid writes with clarity and candor... rather than cluttering a complex topic with innuendo or vagaries, she concentrates on presenting the essential tenets to understanding the world of the psychic/intuitive. *The Psychic Yellow Brick Road* is a must-read for beginners in the metaphysical arena, students who want to learn to do readings as eventual professionals, and anyone who wants or needs a thorough, lively but gentle key to opening the door to the mysteries that are 'Out There.'"

— ANITA MERRICK
Certified Tarot Master, Psychic Medium, and Author of *A Bitter Wind*

CONTENTS

Part One:
PSYCHIC BOOT CAMP

Part Two:
THE INS AND OUTS OF A GENERAL SESSION

Part Three:
WHAT TO WATCH OUT FOR

Part Four:
WORKING WITH ANGELS AND SPIRIT GUIDES

Part Five:
WHAT TO EXPECT WITH MEDIUMSHIP

And Finally:
CAN I DO THIS TOO?

FOREWORD

"You've always had the power..."

~ GLINDA THE GOOD WITCH

When Corbie called to tell me the title and tagline of this book, I was enchanted. I think I even clicked my heels together three times.

As a fellow writer, publisher, marketer, and evidential psychic medium, I've often discussed with Corbie how we wished clients knew more of metaphysics so they could get the most from their sessions. Now they can.

We've also lamented the psychic snake oil sales folks, and wished there was a great and powerful guide to help folks better discern the good psychics from the charlatans who we'd really like someone to drop a house on. Now there is.

Corbie's book, *The Psychic Yellow Brick Road: How to Find the Real Wizards and Avoid the Flying Monkeys*, is a healing Baum, uh, balm in the tornado of psychic misinformation flying around bookshelves everywhere. The internet is no better. Computer screens are the curtains from behind which self-appointed Ozzes speak—many of whom you should ignore.

To date, I've read for well over 20,000 clients. Corbie's numbers are even greater. Further, Corbie is one of the featured channels in Robert Schwartz's breakthrough, bestselling series, *Your Soul's Plan*, and *Your Soul's Gift*. This all adds up to one tremendous case study. The sheer volume of data Corbie's gathered is pure gold.

Drawing from decades of her successful and celebrated psychic service to this world, Corbie's created a five-curtain call finale of psychic reading FAQs. Clients, as well as beginning and professional intuitives, can benefit from this body of work. It is *the* Yellow Brick Road to all your heart's truest desires.

Clients can find clarity and deep insight on questions that are most often asked. They can also learn how to work arm in arm with their chosen psychic medium/channel and the spirit world. With this knowledge (and a good psychic!), Corbie's book can help make readings a pivotal, life-changing event—especially if the client can discover they're psychic, too!

Beginning psychics will find a wealth of sage wisdom to tuck in their toolbox. Honest, easy to understand, and based on real all-over-the-world experience, *The Psychic Yellow Brick Road: How to Find the Real Wizards and Avoid the Flying Monkeys* should be one of the first "introduction to psychic work" books you buy.

Professional psychics can learn from a colleague who continues to prosper in her dream career— perhaps, most importantly, a full-time metaphysician who creates success in any venue. From traveling the show circuit to working with internet services to creating her own social media following and audience, Corbie's been over many rainbows.

It is my sincere honor to write this foreword. Corbie Mitleid is one of the real wizards out there. I urge you to book a reading or, at the least, buy this book. Let Corbie help you remember:

> *"Home is a place we all must find, child. It's not just a place where you eat or sleep. Home is knowing. Knowing your mind, knowing your heart, knowing your courage. If we know ourselves, we're always home, anywhere."*

> ~ Glinda the Good Witch

BERNADETTE CARTER-KING
Professional Psychic Medium and
Owner/CEO of Building Beautiful Souls, Inc.
(www.buildingbeautifulsouls.com)

A THOUGHT
ABOUT GOD

In *The Psychic Yellow Brick Road*, we use the term
"God" to name the Central Point, the Immanence,
the Creator. Some people use the term "Goddess." Some use the word "Spirit." Others may say
"Source" or "All That Is." Any and all of these are
correct if they are right for YOU, and can/should
substitute for the word "God" as you read. Don't let
a label diminish the message, or pull you away from
your immersion in the book.

Basically, God (in whatever form) owns the grocery store and doesn't care if you come in through
the deli (Goddess), health and beauty aids (Spirit),
floral (All That Is) or any other department. You're
just welcome to shop and find nourishment and
value. Period.

INTRODUCTION

I've gotten to live my dream career—though I got there in a roundabout way. When I was nine, I read a book called *The Witch Family* by Eleanor Estes. Instead of thinking *Oooh, that's scary,* or *Ha ha ha,* my only thought was, *And your point is?* I knew there was magic in the world, and I wanted to find it for myself.

Fast forward to 1973. I was a high school senior in Cherry Hill, New Jersey, working part time at Spencer Gifts. It was the year *Live and Let Die* came out— with Roger Moore as James Bond and newcomer Jane Seymour as Solitaire, the mysterious card reader. Spencer's carried the James Bond 007 Tarot Deck, and I bought it. Besides, we were ALL hippies then— a tarot deck was required, right along with fringed jackets and elephant-leg bell bottoms.

It wasn't long before a lot of people moved on to disco and roller blades, but I stayed with the Tarot. I read for friends for many years, working to keep myself a clear channel for useful information. That meant not arguing mentally with what I was getting intuitively, and keeping my ego out of the way. In other words, while I might not agree with the information I was getting if I was in such a situation, I trusted that Spirit knew it was the right message for the person receiving the reading. And I made sure I remembered that I was just the instrument Spirit was using to get Its point across; all credit went to the Folks Upstairs.

Though it wasn't my intention, all that clearing out made room for Spirit to help me "up my game." In 1994, working on some past life investigations proved to be a catalyst for my own abilities. Without formal instruction of any kind, I found myself able to do hands-on healing work, perform distance energy work over the phone, and act as a liaison between discarnate entities and those of us currently in a body. Spirit gave me the "assignment" of being a doorway Home for souls caught in the Grey Spaces—the place where those who have died wander if they cannot find the Light on their own. And I found I had a talent for channeling souls and Higher Selves for those who need to know the hows and whys of their life challenges. That's when I hung out my professional shingle part time.

I still kept one foot in the "real world" for another seven years, with jobs as diverse as a legal assistant, graphic novel writer, video producer, voiceover talent and executive recruiter. But when my husband Carle and I watched the towers burn on 9/11, I turned to him and said: "I *must* do the psychic work full time. People need to know there are other answers than the ones the world gives them." Carle replied: "I believe in you. Go do it." And, thus, I started my full-time career as an intuitive counselor and psychic medium.

What I do now uses a combination of those un-expected gifts and the more accessible tools I've found useful over the years. I continue to hone my intuitive skills; my certifications are a testimony to the ongoing work. My goal is to continue living the "Examined Life," not only to learn more techniques, but also going within myself to eradicate fears, bias, judgment, ego—anything that can get in the way of unconditional love and compassion.

The Psychic Yellow Brick Road shares a bit of what I've learned over the past forty years in the meta-physical realm: what intuitives can and cannot do, how to get the best from your session, and how to keep yourself safe from charlatans, scam artists, and well-meaning but misguided readers. We look at some of the typical questions people ask. We touch on subjects like spirit guides, angels, and medium-ship. And, when it comes right down to it, you'll see that YOU can learn to do this work, too.

Ready? Go find your ruby slippers, and I'll dig out my magic wand.

Part One:

PSYCHIC BOOT CAMP

This section is made up of the most basic information needed before you wade into the world of Metaphysics. It is designed to keep you safe from the charlatans, give you a clearer idea of what you can (and cannot) expect, and prepare you to get the most out of every session.

PSYCHICS 101:

The Good, The Bad, and The Cleos

Back in the 1990s, when pay-per-call psychics were becoming all the rage, there was a woman known as Miss Cleo. She claimed to be from Jamaica but was actually from East Los Angeles. She made extravagant promises regarding the information she and her fellow psychics would give you when none of them had the faintest idea of what real psychic readings were supposed to be. And she became notorious as the face for phony phone psychics, who were trained to offer you vagaries, promise to lift curses, and generally convince you to spend a lot more money than you wanted (or they merited). She is the "Cleo" in the title of this chapter, and the inspiration for the whole darn book.

These days, I do my healing and spiritual work in several forums—not only on my own website and through in-person appointments, but also through other psychic websites and psychic fairs. That's how I discovered a very disturbing fact: most people have only the vaguest idea of what a psychic does—what they are SUPPOSED to do—and how to recognize the good ones.

Let me share with you some of the ins-and-outs—or, as my generation might say, let's all read *Dick and Jane Go See A Psychic.*

There are as many ideas on *how* to choose a good psychic as there are psychics. Some insist that if a psychic doesn't immediately tell you something they could not have known, they aren't a "genuine" psychic. Others tell you to deliberately project incorrect or misrepresentational thoughts at the psychic; they believe that "real" psychics will know when your thoughts aren't the truth. Then there's a group of people with the exact opposite opinion: if the Universe led you to the psychic, they HAVE to be the right one for you to see, no matter how odd you feel around them.

As someone who has both been consulted by other psychics and consulted them for my own intuitive business for decades, I can assure you that NONE of the ideas in that last paragraph will get you a psychic you can trust, or an experience that you'll find useful.

I want to start off by giving you valuable insights on how to select a psychic or spiritual intuitive. You'll discover what these professionals can and can't do. And, lastly, you'll learn how to use the information once you've got it.

STEP 1: *Deciding What Type of Psychic You Want to Consult.*

Not all psychics are the same—just as doctors, teachers, or artists are unique within their professions based on specialties and personal talents. A doctor can be a specialist of the heart, lungs, or feet. A teacher can teach math, Spanish, or history. An artist can work in oils, watercolors, or marble.

The fact is that not all psychics use the same methods or have skills in the same field. Does that make one more genuine than another? Not in the least. After all, the fact that a math teacher is unable to substitute for a Spanish class doesn't make them less of a teacher, does it?

Some (but not all) of the methodologies that reputable psychics can use include Tarot, oracle card decks, runes, crystals, I Ching, numerology, astrology, palm reading, aura reading, chakra work, angel connections, energy healing, dream interpretation, past life readings, channeling, mediumship, pendulum work, phrenology, and spirit art, with more techniques coming forward every day.

Once you decide what issues you'd like to address with the intuitive you choose, you will probably be able to home in on which methods you'd like for them to utilize. It will pay off, in the long run, to familiarize yourself with the various systems we've named above; there may be one or two that you are especially drawn to, and that knowledge will assist you in focusing your search.

Step 2: *We're Off to Find the Psychic... (apologies to Dorothy and the Wizard!)*

In these "interesting times," it is easier to find a psychic—or, at least, one who bills themselves as such—than ever before. Chat lines, 900 numbers, websites, local periodicals, you name it—we intuitives are out there! The sheer number can be confusing and a little daunting.

There are several things to look for when choosing your psychic. Using the mnemonic **PSYCHIC**, we've provided seven simple rules to help you remember them:

> **P**rofessionalism
>
> **S**haring references
>
> **Y**ou are in control of your own destiny
>
> **C**harges
>
> **H**ere, I can fix anything...for a price
>
> **I**nappropriate actions
>
> **C**onnections

Rule 1: Professionalism. The psychic you choose should *be* and *act like* a professional. This does not mean that they have to make a full time living at such work. However, they should respect others in their field, your time and energy as a client, and adhere to generally accepted social behaviors.

If you needed a lawyer, how would you decide which one should handle your case? You'd choose one who answered your questions, gave you references if you wanted them, and told you exactly what the work would cost you (including how such costs were structured). You'd prefer one who didn't patronize you or try to intimidate you into using their services. You'd want the ability to make appointments in a reasonable amount of time, the assurance that such appointments would be kept, and the knowledge that you wouldn't have to cool your heels for hours after you arrived. You'd hope to receive clear "layman's explanations" regarding any terms or events you didn't understand. You'd expect your business to be kept private and not discussed with other clients. Overall, you'd expect to be treated with courtesy and respect—not as a supplicant, not as an ignorant simpleton, and not as "money on two feet."

And that's what you should expect from your psychic as well. *No exceptions.*

Rule 2: Sharing references. If you found your potential psychic through a source other than word-of-mouth, it is perfectly legitimate of you to ask for references. As long as there is no breaking of confidences, you should be able to speak with three or four people who have availed themselves of the psychic's services.

Some good questions you can ask:

* Were you comfortable with this person?

* Did they charge fairly?

* Was the information you received accurate and/or useful? Why or why not?

* How hard is it to get an appointment?

* Did they try to sell all kinds of "extras" (mojo bags, spell candles, curse-breakers, etc.)?

* Would you go back to this person again?

One of the reasons that you need more than one or two conversations is to see whether the psychic harps on the same themes all the time. Are they always talking about failing relationships, or dark futures, or devious connections? Then, more than likely, there's a fair amount of those types of activities in the psychic's personal life—which just might be coloring their views. Conversely, if all a psychic ever gives is "sweetness and light" with no shadings of challenge or growth, then they either cannot or will not see that life has both blessings *and* tests. Life is not a fairy tale; it's not happily ever after every time. Honesty, tempered with tact and neutrality, is the mark of a clear-channel psychic.

Three or four conversations like this should give you a fairly accurate view of the psychic in question.

Rule 3: You are in control of your own destiny. There's a famous old acronym: FEAR = False Evidence Appearing Real. No psychic should try to convince you that they see your death, that you are cursed, that you have bad luck, that events in your life are totally out of your control, or that someone else (most likely, the psychic) must help you out of your dire predicament. If someone starts feeding you information that makes you doubt yourself, your life, or your state of mind, LEAVE.

On the other hand, if the psychic does not give you "everything is sweetness and light," but points out difficulties and challenges ahead—that may be what they truly see and, therefore, it's appropriate to alert you. They may even go further by suggesting several ways for you to direct your life, or actions to help you make the best of such situations, or point out the likely unfolding if you take this path or that. Take such advice the way you would anyone else's; see if it resonates with you. If it does, then act upon it. If it feels neutral or "off," then feel free to ignore it or shelve it for a period of time. That, my friends, is what free will is all about!

With every rule, of course, there is an exception: if you really DON'T like what you hear, but it keeps nibbling at you—both during and after the session—it could be that you are being pointed in one of those directions that provides growth. And, if you are confronted by some useful but vile-tasting medicine, it might be to your advantage to screw up your nose and take it. Reconsider the session information seriously after a week or two; try to be objective about it and listen to your own intuition. You may find that it has settled into something you want to act upon.

Rule 4: Charges. Psychics can charge as little as $10 and as much as—well, as the traffic will bear. Internationally famous psychics can charge thousands of dollars. Generally, psychics can run somewhere between $10 to $200 for a set price or may charge "by the minute." For instance, $1 per minute figures out to $60 per hour, and the psychic only charges for the time in session with you.

Because you have requested a service from the psychic in question, they do deserve to get paid if they are at all courteous, reasonable, and relatively on target. Notice, I say "relatively." No one is 100 percent accurate; they, like the rest of us, are merely human. But if they are clearly doing their best for you, remember that they are offering a service—just like a doctor, a plumber, or a master chef. As in any other profession, for a psychic to ask for fair compensation is not wrong. Think of it as merely exchanging your energy (payment) for the psychic's (their abilities, time, and focus on you).

Rule 5: Here, I can fix anything...for a price. Here we come to those soi-disant ("so-called") psychics who prey on those who feel powerless about their own lives. Countless times I've heard of someone paying thousands of dollars to have a hex lifted, to chase away an evil spirit, to get rid of a rival, to force another person to fall in love with them, to cause misfortune to a perceived enemy, or to pick magic numbers that will win the Irish Sweepstakes. The reasons are endless and, sad to say, there are folks in the psychic business solely for the money and the power. (That can be true in any profession, but in one as little understood as psychic work, the opportunities to bilk the innocent are enormous.)

If, my friend, you come away from this chapter with one piece of information fixed in your minds, make it this: YOU are the one who can heal your own life, meet your own challenges, and clear your own karma—no one else. Karmically, you do not have the right to "force" another's will: to fall in love with you, to give you money, to do anything. You are only in charge of your life. (Most of us have our hands full with that anyway!) And, by extension, the psychic who promises to fix your life with candles, mojo bags, hex powder, floor washes or the like, is assuming that your free will is theirs for the taking.

Prove them wrong!

I want to extend a caveat here. There are many honest, talented and dedicated Wiccans and other practicing pagans who work with candle rituals, herbs, etc. These good folk are not included in this caution. The reputable ones will generally show you how to work with such things while teaching you how to engage your will in the matter; do not assume that they are going to do everything for you while you pour coins in their purses. In this case, the objects they suggest for use are merely *your* tools. Your will is still what makes them work.

Rule 6: Inappropriate actions. We've gone over some of the lesser of these: psychics trying to sell you services you don't need, and psychics trying to convince you that they, and ONLY they, know the answers to your life's challenges. But there are other actions of a darker and more sinister kind.

As one of my sister psychics says, "a muddy channel will carry muddy water." As your psychic channels information to you, make sure they are not muddied by fundamentalist thinking, an overwhelming ego, negative energies regarding their own lives, or just plain amoral greed.

What is considered an inappropriate action? Anything where the psychic tries to insinuate themselves into your life, your finances, or your personal information.

Examples:

* The psychic tries to convince you that some part of your finances, jewelry, or other items of worth are "cursed" and the only way to "clear" them is for the psychic to take them over for a period (these can include wills, deeds or other legal papers).

* The psychic tries to convince you of some kind of Karmic connection they have with you, and therefore you MUST become their student, or support them, or otherwise wrap your life around theirs.

* The psychic tries to convince you that your ways of thinking (religion, beliefs, etc.) are damning, and that you MUST change them on peril of your soul—and that they have the *only* answer that will save you.

* The psychic takes advantage of your instability regarding a relationship and "makes moves" on you; this is sexual predation, pure and simple.

You can see where we're heading...metaphysicians and spiritual intuitives of any repute know that, first and foremost, we are all entitled to our free will. No one may take it from us without incurring some serious Karmic debt. So, if someone tries to convince you that you're on the road to perdition, and they're the only vehicle to take you away from all this, run—from them, under your own power, and immediately.

Rule 7: Connections. Connections are what using a psychic is all about: connections with your inner guides, connections with the paths you need for growth, connections with people and things you can trust. The inner connection you forge with a reputable psychic is a valuable one that, in the very best of circumstances, will be of mutual benefit.

Even if you do everything we've discussed above, the last and most important key to choosing your psychic is going to be gauging how you feel. Is there is a sense of neutrality? Are you open to what they say, but not invested in them before the meeting? Do you get a feeling of, "Yes, this is a person I want to connect my energies with?" Then, it's a safe bet that your experience with the psychic will good for you. If, at any time before you sit down with them, you feel a twinge of "ehhh, maybe not" then HONOR that intuition! Keep looking. There are enough of us out there for you to hit the bull's eye on trust.

And, now, take that connection one step further. If you feel that you've been treated fairly by the psychic you've chosen or if you feel the information is rational, relevant, and useful to you, then make connections with your friends. Let them know that you have a psychic you trust and find reputable.

Face it: we intuitives aren't exactly able to advertise on prime-time TV or radio—and even cable has been taken up by people touting the latest shady phone psychic sites. The best way for us to continue our work is for positive word-of-mouth reporting to come from our clients. This helps build the bridges of trust all the way around.

PSYCHICS 102:

How to Prepare for a Great Psychic Session

In the last chapter, we discussed what a psychic can and cannot do, how to tell a good one from a bad one, and how you can use the information from a psychic session once you have it.

In **Psychics 102**, you'll learn how to prepare yourself for a good reading: what questions to ask, what parameters to set, where your mindset should be to have the best and most useful experience, and ways to utilize the information you receive. As in Psychics 101, we have a simple mnemonic, or "word key," that will outline all the steps you need. You're looking for answers? Use the word **ANSWER** to keep yourself on target:

Accept responsibility for your part in the session

No pop quizzes, no comparisons

State your intentions clearly
Widen your horizons
Evaluate your information
Respond to the Universe

Rule 1: Accept responsibility for your part in the session. The most important thing you can take into any psychic appointment is an acceptance of responsibility. You are ultimately responsible for your reading because it's your attitude that determines whether this will be a useful meeting or merely an opportunity for a few giggles. This is known as "fluff begets fluff." If you come into a session expecting nothing, that's most often what you'll get. Why? You have a preconceived notion that nothing the psychic says to you will matter, so you tend to dismiss information as coincidental or think, *Someone must have told the psychic,* or *They say the same thing to everyone.*

If you're not focused, the psychic can find it hard to get into what you want to know. It's like a mother trying to direct a child who has no interest in the eventual destination but finds every reason in the book (and a few new ones) to avoid getting there. Eventually, Mom gives up and takes Junior home— destination never reached.

The best psychic sessions are the ones where you see yourself as a true co-creator in the process. When you are more open, interested, and focused, you are a better subject for your intuitive professional—and the better your results will be.

Also, STAY SOBER. I cannot stress this enough. When your bloodstream is carrying alcohol or drugs, your mental processes get fuzzy. You can't concentrate on what is happening, nor truly understand what we tell you. And we're likely to pick up what isn't there on a normal, day-to-day basis. Think of it as psychic pink elephants: the drunk sees them, and no one else does. When we read you, and you're under the influence, we're looking through your mental lenses. If they're fogged, we can't see either.

Rule 2: No pop quizzes, no comparisons. Let's say you're an architect. You're at a first meeting with your new client. You get there, expecting to have an honest and useful give-and-take so you can provide good and expert service. But when you arrive, the client sits down and says: "You're an architect. Prove it. Sketch out my dream house without me telling you anything." Or imagine getting there and, based on preliminary information the client has provided, you bring plans for a sustainable house in the country. When you unroll your blueprints, the client says "You're not a real architect. Couldn't you tell I really wanted a refurbished brownstone?"

Playing "test the psychic" is useless and demeaning to both of you. Giving us incorrect information about your circumstances and expecting us to recognize its fabrication, or saying "tell me something you couldn't know and I'll have a reading with you" is like asking us to roll over and fetch! We're proud of what we do, glad to be in service to the world, and happy to help you. But only if you treat us with the same respect you'd treat any other professional whose services you need.

Part of your pre-appointment responsibility is to check out the psychic ahead of time—either through personal referrals, reading through their testimonial books at a public event, or reviewing their website. If you don't get a good feeling or are unsure this is the psychic you want to trust with your important questions, then don't go to them. Wait until you come across someone whose credentials say enough to you that you're willing to sit down with them on an honest basis. Not every psychic is right for every person, and we're aware of that; if we're not right for you, another intuitive will be at another time.

Some clients feel a need to name drop and compare during a meeting. When you begin your session by saying you've been to (or read) Sylvia Browne, Sonia Choquette, John Edward, James Van Praagh, and half the psychics at Lily Dale—and start telling the psychic everything *they* said—it highlights four issues: 1) you've looked to an awful lot of psychics for answers and still feel you haven't gotten what you need, 2) you might be "shopping" for a psychic that will give you the answers you WANT to hear and will accept nothing less, 3) it tells your current psychic that any information given in this session will likely be compared on an inequitable basis (the information might have been gained during a private session, gallery event or something you read in their book that merely *sounded* like your situation, although it was not channeled specifically for you), and 4) you're coming into the session with pre-conceived notions rather than an open mind.

A by-product of bringing up other psychics' information in the session is that you may derail the intuitive you're with. In my case, when I am channeling someone's past lives, I am completely focused on the vision; it runs like a movie in my head. If a client is constantly interrupting with "Madame Hoohah never told me that" or "Swami Swellanda said I'd been with my husband for my past fifty-seven lives" or even "No, I don't think so," I lose the reception, lose the movie, and am pulled abruptly out of the Akashic Records, the dimension where all lives are stored. I am catapulted back to the Here and Now.

It's often difficult to get back to the same book in the Library for you after such a break in communication. The best advice is simply to hear out the psychic and reserve your questions for a more appropriate point in the reading. Questions are good things, but get all the information on the table first.

Rule 3: State your intentions clearly. How many times have you gone to a psychic, and an hour after the session realized there were a lot of questions you forgot to ask? Saying to us, "just tell me what you see about my future" means that we scan everything ahead. And there's only so much ground we can cover in a session.

Therefore, as part of your prep-work, you really need to know what you want to know. This is not quite like coming in with preconceived notions; instead, doing prep-work sets up a structure for the session that is most useful to both you and your intuitive.

How do you do that?

First, understand why you are asking for a session. If it's to clear confusion about direction, that's one kind of reading. If it's how to handle the dynamics of a situation and the people involved, that's a second. If it's choosing among several options, that's a third. And so on. When you pinpoint the underlying "kink in the pipeline," then we know what to pull out of our Psychic Toolbox for you.

Your next job is to outline and prioritize your questions. As my clients know, I joke about being a "Noo Yawker" and, therefore, talking very fast means our sessions are packed (and it's why you get a recording of our time together, so you can review things later on). Still, if you have a lot of questions about many areas of your life, we might not get to it all in the time allotted. Therefore, make sure you know which subjects are most important (family or work), and then decide the question within the category (Will my mother-in-law have to live with us? Is our company going to be merged? If that happens, what will that do to my job?).

Finally, specific questions are better than general questions. It's part of that sub-grouping idea. To use the relocation scenario: if you ask about relocation, in general, I may see opportunities in Denver or San Jose. That doesn't help if your company has only offered you positions in Altoona, Savannah, and Houston! If there are definite parameters within which we have to work, tell us. The less time backtracking, because we're guessing about the immutable factors, the more information we can pack into our time with you.

Rule 4: Widen your horizons. You wouldn't be human if you didn't come into a session with answers you hope to get. *("Please say that Doug is Mr. Right." "Tell me that my boss will promote me."*

"You've got to predict that my finances are going to get better this year.") If you want certain answers, and you think they absolutely have to be structured in a certain way, then it makes it impossible to help you get past your challenges.

Resist the urge to "yes, but." If I see that your mother-in-law will be instrumental in helping you get your down payment for the house you want, don't say, "But she always gives money to everyone else in the family except us" or "But she'll make us pay for it with all her carping; she always does when she lends us anything." This defeats the purpose two ways: you are dismissing the idea that circumstances or people can change, and you're focusing on the negative. (What we focus on is what we get—a basic Law of Attraction rule!)

If a psychic sees something happening, they won't necessarily give you all the details, because the situation remains fluid. Leave room for circumstances to unfold in the best way possible (and visualize it that way!). And if a situation looks like it's going to differ from your expectations, leave room for a changed mind.

When you formulate questions either before your session, or based on information during the reading, it's more useful to ask "how" rather than "yes/no" questions. If you ask, "Will I get a new job?" and the psychic says "no," then you have no place to go—and you've turned your free will over to the psychic.

A far better question would be "What do I need to do to get a new job?" That kind of questioning enables us to share tools to help you explore where to look, avoid pitfalls and consider possibilities, determine what kind of job you are truly suited for and discover those in your circle who might help you up the corporate ladder. You get a full toolbox, and you can go out and create your own life. Free will, as I'll always remind you, is everything!

It's the same with a question like "Will I get into college?" It's better to ask "how" and also to list the places to which you've applied. For example, someone could get admitted to Ohio State, Georgia Tech, and Lehigh. However, one may signal a change in major while there. One may be a short two-year stint. And one may open the doorway to a chosen career—one year early. Asking "how" questions help you explore know all your options.

And, finally, an answer to a specific question may show you just how absurd your question was in the first place. Laugh; don't be upset with yourself (or the psychic). We're on your side.

Rule 5: Evaluate your information. Even if you've been going to the same intuitive for years and you think you know how they read, delayed understanding is common. And if it's a first time, then you definitely need time to digest what you've been told. It's why I tell you to always get a recording.

Let's say you and your daughter are always at loggerheads, and you never get to know what's going on in her head. What may not make sense to you today ("your daughter will ask you to help her through a personal crisis, and you have to be gentle with her") becomes crystal clear to you in four months, when a friend of hers dies in a car accident, she's picked for a semester in Barcelona and she's never been away from home, or a sports injury means she loses a basketball scholarship to college.

Sometimes you will get what I term a "verification reading." If I, a stranger (or at least someone who doesn't interact with you on a day to day basis) tell you in our session precisely what you were thinking about doing but hadn't discussed with anyone else, those are your spirit guides and angels giving you the thumbs-up about the accuracy of your thoughts and decisions. If a psychic doesn't give you a whole bunch of information you don't already know, it's because what you know is what you should act upon, plain and simple.

And accept that you may come to your session with all kinds of plans about where you are going to move, and yet the cards or your spirit guides insist on telling you that your Significant Other will not be in the picture in another few months' time. You may want to hear about your children, but the cards discuss your health options. Know that your spirit guides and angels, in this case, are following the old Rolling Stones' axiom: "You can't always get what you want...but you get what you need."

Rule 6: Respond to the Universe. Now that you've had your session and you have all these new facts and factors to consider, what do you do? It's vital that you view the information as neutral. What you do with it determines its usefulness.

If you find out that your husband has been keeping some work problems from you, rather than panicking about it *("Why won't he talk to me? Does he want a divorce? Is he going to lose his job?"),* see if you can get some feedback from him.

If you ask a question about finances and the Tower shows up in your reading, which generally foresees a crisis or a breakdown of some kind, don't sit up all night worrying! Make a point of investigating where you stand financially. Start your priority list about what's important to you and what isn't. See the information as a heads-up that this aspect of your life needs attention. And if it turns out that yes, you do lose your house or your partner leaves you or you don't get the job you wanted, remember that none of these have to be disasters forever—or even immediately. Always look at a problem and say "Next? Now where do I go?" rather than dwelling on what happened.

It's also not uncommon to find out that losing your house means you move to a neighborhood better suited to you and your children... your partner leaving you makes room for a real Soulmate to walk into your life... and not getting the job you wanted propels you into opening the small business you've been dreaming about, but could never make happen as long as you were comfy in your job security!

If the information you receive in session isn't what you wanted, resist the impetus to go to another psychic to try and get the answer you were looking for. That doesn't work, on a couple of levels. If you want to hear something that badly, you will eventually find a psychic who knows that, is less than scrupulous, and tells you what you want to hear with a "hook" to get you coming back again and again. You are wasting a whole lot of money looking for what doesn't exist. And the truthful information you may have gotten eventually gets muddied and forgotten in the process.

Along that train of thought, don't return to your psychic month after month hoping the answer will change if you haven't worked with the information from your last session with them. We're not gurus—we're mentors at best. An honest intuitive will, if you keep coming back for session after session with the same questions, finally decline to read you further.

And lastly, remember that a psychic and their information are tools for you to use to make your life what you want it to be. We, in and of ourselves, are not the repairman. No matter what we tell you, it's up to you to make the best life you can with the building blocks that God, your Higher Self, and your spirit guides have lined up for you.

Keep the "ANSWER" in mind, and every session with your intuitive will be a beneficial one!

PAY FAIR TO
PLAY FAIR

I love doing psychic fairs, spiritual expos, and holistic events. They are a great way for me to make contact with people who may not live close to me, but who want to sit with me for a Tarot reading, or mediumship, or to contact spirit guides or angels. They may not be able to do an entire Soul Plan reading with me, but they do want to touch in with their past lives. And they really do want to see what a psychic medium does "up close and personal."

There's a great deal that goes into a show appearance that most people don't think about. There's the booth fee (anywhere between $150 and $1,000, depending on the venue and the length of the show). Then there's the hotel. And paying my front person. And gas, tolls, and food. It's not just the financial overhead that gets factored in, either. There are other dynamics in play. Being away from the husband I love for ten to twelve days every month has its own emotional tariff. Now add in the years I have spent learning my craft, the courses I have taken, the sheer number of people I read for every year (it's well over 1,000) and the energy it takes for me to see person after person for anywhere from eight to eleven hours a day.

Yes, that's right: up to eleven hours a day at my booth. When I do a show, I am there to work. I share answers, bring in people from the Other Side, help with questions on romance, finances, career, spiritual roads, life paths, and all the things that we humans have to deal with on our "everyday tour bus." I rarely take a break. It is far more important to me that I sit with my client and focus on them with compassion and care—to bring them the best psychic reading experience I can. And to go from client to client to client, with complete focus, complete compassion, constantly reaching into the Aethers, to spirit guides and those on the Other Side, using far more senses than just the usual five—trust me, at the end of show day I am completely exhausted, no matter how much I've enjoyed the proceedings.

All that said, I do charge for my readings. The pricing I have set for my appointments is fair, and generally in line with other practitioners who have my skill set and level of experience. At the same time, there are always those people who come to me and say one of five things:

"How about doing a reading for less? At least you're getting paid."

"Can my friend and I have a reading together and only pay for one?"

"Here, do a free reading for me and if I'm impressed I'll tell all my friends about you."

"Wow. That's a lot. But I really want a reading." (Stands there, watches me, waiting for me to offer them a deal.)

"Why won't you give me a free reading? You're just greedy. You're not very spiritual." (Yes, to my face.)

None of these are going to get what they're asking for. Why? Because they are asking me to value myself, my training, and my time LESS, just because they didn't want to pay a fair wage for the services offered. They are attempting to guilt me, bully me, or wheedle me into taking less for my services.

If we want to think about this carefully, let's switch the profession in each case and see how that sounds:

To the hair stylist: "How about doing a cut for less money? At least you're not standing around."

To the plumber: "How about you change the pipes in my bathroom sink *and* replace my dishwasher, but I only pay for one service call?"

To the cleaner: "Clean my house a couple of times for free; if I think it's good enough, I'll tell everyone how good you are."

To the dress shop owner: "Wow, that's a lot for that dress. But I really want it for my party." (Stop. Stare. Wait.)

To the physician: "Why won't you see me for free? You'd rather I just got sick and died. You're not very compassionate."

These examples aren't so far-fetched. In each one, the person who wants the services is trying guilt, manipulation, vague promises or outright wheeling-and-dealing to underpay for a service that has a set price.

While I respect bargaining in some situations (there are actually some cultures where you are EX-PECTED to haggle), a psychic event is not one of them. And the more time you waste trying to get me to lower my price, the less time I have to take care of clients who are standing there, willing to pay fairly, and respect both my time and theirs. So generally, I will just ignore you—and I'm certainly not inclined to give you a cut-rate appointment.

For those who accuse me of never doing a pro bono (Latin for "for the good") reading: trust me, I do. If someone comes up to me respectfully and asks about my services and simply says they don't have the money that day, Spirit will sometimes nudge me and whisper, "This one needs you." And I always heed that whisper from Heaven. To such a person, I may say, "Look, I can't read you here at a discount, but this I will do. If you call me on (this day) at (this time), I'll read you for free." I can do that ten times in a weekend, and it's a certainty that only one or two will make the effort to call me at the time specified. That's because they truly needed my guidance. The rest? Could care less; if they didn't feel like they got a "win" in the situation by getting me to lower my price, they can't be bothered to contact me later.

So, when you are going to a psychic fair, remember these rules:

ONE: The admission price (usually somewhere between $5 and $20) just gets you in the door. There may be several lectures for you to go to which are included in the admission price. You are welcome to "window shop" the psychics and vendors who are at the event, and they will all probably be more than happy to answer questions regarding the services they provide, the products they sell, and how they came to be in that segment of the metaphysical business world. But the admission price generally does not include a reading.

TWO: Unless you have a specific psychic medium you really want to see, take your time. Visit each booth. Take a look at the setup and what is on/around the table.

THREE: Talk directly to the psychic medium if you can, but if they are busy doing a reading, please don't interrupt them (would you want to have someone interrupt YOUR Tarot reading?). If they have an assistant, or a "front person," talk to them. Otherwise read the information available in the form of brochures, signs, or the testimonial books. These will give you a feel for their skill level, their specialties, their client interaction, and how people felt after their session at the table.

FOUR: Lastly, remember that you are putting out your hard-earned money. If the psychic doesn't feel like they are intelligent, honest, or truly engaged in supporting and empowering the client, don't go to that person. Save that money for a psychic medium that will sincerely and actively support your quest to make your life more fulfilling, abundant and joyful.

A reading is a two-way street paved with mutual respect, professionalism, and willingness to engage. Remember that your "fair pay" equals the psychic's "fair play," and everyone leaves the session respected and empowered.

WHEN GETTING A READING WON'T HELP

You'd think this was the LAST thing a psychic or intuitive would say to you: "Don't have a reading with me!" But there are times when a divination session with a psychic won't get you the answers you need or support you in ways that serve you best. There are also classic behaviors that a professional psychic will see and refuse to become involved with. Some of the situations may seem ludicrous to you ("I would never do that!"); but, trust me, they can and do happen. What might some of these be?

Example 1: The client feels they absolutely MUST hear a certain answer to a question. If this is the case, the client is not open enough to listen to what the Universe wants to tell them. Every psychic intuitive I know can remember countless clients who were so set on having (or keeping) a certain relationship, or not having to face the consequences of a difficult situation, or wanting their will to override someone else's, that they ask the same question over and over, tilting it ever so slightly to see if they can get us to give them the answer they want. Here's an example of that kind of manipulation:

CLIENT: *Does Bruce think about me?*

PSYCHIC: *No.*

CLIENT: *Has he ever thought about me?*

PSYCHIC: *Not the way you want.*

CLIENT: *If I do [such-and-such] will he think about me?*

PSYCHIC: *No.*

CLIENT: *Is he going to call soon?*

PSYCHIC: *He isn't.*

CLIENT: *Well if he isn't going to call soon, will he call later?*

Notice that this person is so desperate for a relationship with Bruce that she will not accept that it isn't what HE wants, and she would be better off turning her attention elsewhere. She is not listening to what is being said and believes that if she keeps up the relentless demand for reassurance that the exhausted intuitive will finally say "Yes, he loves you and wants seven babies with you, but he just doesn't know it yet."

Example 2: The client is extremely negative/angry about a situation. In this case, the client will not be able to hear how to either change the situation into a win-win or walk away with the lesson the

Universe wants to share with them. Here's a real-life example from one of my Canadian shows years ago:

CLIENT: *Can you tell me where my ex-husband is sleeping with his mistress?*

PSYCHIC: *No, I don't do remote spying.*

CLIENT: *Well, is he with the same one or a different one?*

PSYCHIC: *I don't do remote spying, I'm sorry.*

CLIENT: *How many prostitutes has he cheated on me with?*

PSYCHIC: *That is still remote spying.*

CLIENT: *Oh. Well, is he sick? Is he going to die soon? Can I still get his money?*

Another situation:

CLIENT: *My supervisor at work is mean to me. Is she going to get any nicer?*

PSYCHIC: *No*

CLIENT: *Is her supervisor going to make her stop harassing me?*

PSYCHIC: *No*

CLIENT: *Is she going to fire me?*

PSYCHIC: *No*

CLIENT: *But if she doesn't like people she fires them. Are you sure she won't fire me?*

PSYCHIC: *It doesn't appear so in anything I am seeing.*

CLIENT: *I have a meeting with her tomorrow. Is she going to fire me then, or should I quit first?*

Clearly, both of these people are so emotionally tangled in their difficulties that they will not accept objective information on how to improve things; nor are they willing to listen to what is really happening. And as for the remote spying (defined as reading someone in an emotionally volatile situation who has not asked to be read), it is—in my opinion—both unprofessional and unethical. If John and Susan are dating, each can ask about the other. If they break up, neither one can ask about who the ex-partner is dating because it's no longer their business.

The specific danger here is that unscrupulous charlatans (as with all professions, we have our share) will be able to convince the client that they have bad luck, or there is a curse, or there is a hole in their aura, or there are Karmic knots to untie. Instilling such "false fear" in a vulnerable client can result in the theft of thousands of dollars. Why? Because the charlatan gets the client to believe that the situation cannot be overturned without paying for (what in actuality are) fraudulent acts: burning $100 curse-break candles in the dozens, special rituals that only the fraud can perform for them, and so on.

Example 3: The client is so despondent about life that they refuse to see any hope or positivity that the reading brings. In these cases, it's as if the client wants the intuitive to solidify their worldview that Life is Awful. For example:

CLIENT: *I never have any friends.*

PSYCHIC: *I am seeing new friendships for you in the spring.*

Client: *But they never stay; they always leave me.*

Psychic: *Do you want to look at what can change that?*

Client: *No, why bother. It never works. Why am I so lonely?*

As intuitives, we've chosen our profession because we want to give people hope in their future and tools to make their lives better. If you simply want confirmation that your life is awful, that you deserve it, and that it will never change—there are other places that will prove you right. A professional intuitive's office isn't one of them.

Example 4: The client is so unsure about their own ability to control their life that they come to a psychic too frequently. There is no all-encompassing answer for how often you should seek out an intuitive. Some people get sufficient information and empowerment if they see an intuitive once every couple of years. Some people have an annual visit set up with their chosen psychic. And some seek them out more often; this is appropriate if you have taken the information the intuitive has given you, worked with it, and your life has now moved forward.

For instance, if someone comes to me for one of my entrepreneur readings, and two months later their business is in a different place, and they want to review some new directions, I am completely fine with scheduling another appointment for them.

However, if a client comes to me repeatedly asking the same questions, and I give them the same information as the last session—which they refuse to act on—after three readings, I am like a good bartender: I cut them off. They are wasting their money and their time.

Additionally, if someone comes to their intuitive with constant minutiae and overly-detailed questions, it means they are not willing to do any of their own work—and a session does not serve them. Here's an actual example from a reading I did years ago:

> **CLIENT:** *I need to know what needs to be done to sell our house: what furniture goes and how to sell it, what furniture needs to be bought and where to get it, what rooms to be painted and what colors, what to do with the fireplaces, what to do with kitchen counters and cupboards, what to do with the flooring throughout the house; what to do with the basement and how to decorate it; what to do with the garden/furniture for comfort and resale, and which doors and windows to replace.*

These questions that can absolutely be answered with some logical thought and research into what is working for house sales these days. But the person you should talk to is a real estate agent, not a psychic!

Example 5: Specifically, with regard to mediumship, the client constantly wants to speak with their deceased loved one. This is a little touchy in that I feel if you can connect personally with those on the Other Side, feel free to do so. If they come in for you, then they want the connection too! For example, I often hear from my father—a splendid physician who Crossed Over in 2001, but who apparently enjoys working with me in medical intuitive readings from Upstairs.

However, some clients constantly come back seeking to talk to a spouse or a child because they cannot bear to move on without their loved one in their life. In these cases, they have nothing specific to say to those who have Crossed Over, but just want to know that they are there. The constant and repeated request to speak to their Departed Ones does not allow the person still on Earth to heal from the grief and tears and move forward with life; instead, it keeps the client in a permanent state of mourning.

In those cases, I tell the client I will no longer reach for their Dearly Departed, and gently suggest that they look at why they are so desperate to retain the connection when Karmically there is more life for them to live on their own, with new lessons and possibilities. I encourage them to open their own connections, so that they no longer have to spend money to reach their loved ones so frequently.

I also point out that by consistently seeking to reach their Departed Ones, the client can hold them close to the Earth plane, which tangles up their evolution from personality to Spirit. Once this stage is completed, loved ones can freely choose to make spirit form or sound visitations, inspire memories, or appear in a dream to let us know they continue loving us from the Other Side.

If you read these examples carefully, you will see that they all point to the crucial goal of every good intuitive: we want our clients empowered, not dependent; we want them to be willing to move ahead and learn, not stuck in a particular situation or "pity party." We want to be of true service, not an inappropriate crutch or tool.

So, next time you want a reading, ask yourself these questions: *Am I in the right frame of mind for it? Will, I listen objectively? Do I want answers or mere reassurance that what I want can happen? Am I willing to consider other roads, other choices, or other possibilities? Am I willing to be responsible for my own life or do I want someone to "fix" everything for me?*

If you can answer those questions honestly—if you come to see us because you want to move ahead in your life and you want to learn how to make the best of what you have—then we are absolutely delighted to be a part of your Earthwalk. And we welcome the chance to be part of your explorations.

Part Two:

THE INS AND OUTS OF A GENERAL SESSION

This section will help you understand the importance of questions vs. answers during a psychic session. You'll learn what to ask (and which questions won't help you). We'll explain how to understand the answers you're given, and how to ascertain whether those answers are too vague, too detailed, or just plain NOT what will assist you in making your life the best it can be.

CAN A PSYCHIC REALLY READ YOU OVER THE PHONE?

> *I have always been afraid to get a reading over the phone from a psychic. All the 900 number scams—how can they really tell you anything if they can't see you?*
>
> — JEANNIE

I get this question all the time, and it makes me smile. Let me put it to you this way: If I, as a professional psychic, can only read you in person, how do you know I am not merely reading your body language?

Remember that what we are reading is ENERGY: energy in the Akashic records, energy in your energy field, the energy of possibility. And such things can be read anywhere, at any time. I have clients all over the world, and often I will do readings for them based only on information such as birth name and birth date, or a series of questions. And these readings are every bit as accurate as one I might do for them in person—because "energy" has no limitations, physical or otherwise: it is everywhere, all the time.

I admit that I prefer doing mediumship in person because my style has a bit of what I call "heavenly charades." I allow the deceased to give me information through a series of predetermined (by me) physical signals. For instance, they might mime smoking a cigarette if they were a smoker. They might slick their hair back exaggeratedly (a signal for my male deceased ones to kid about being "so handsome!"). Miming the pulling back of a curtain may mean that, at the end, they were conscious at the moment of death—and literally saw the curtain of Heaven pulled aside. A hand over the mouth might mean that they were intubated, on oxygen, or having great trouble breathing in their last days, and so on. But that doesn't mean that I can't do mediumship by phone—I have, often. And it has been successful virtually every time (virtually because, as I often say, even the best intuitive is only 85 percent accurate; the only one 100 percent accurate is God, and He's not doing phone readings as far as I know).

But here is your biggest clue: every single reading done by every single channel and medium in *both* of Robert Schwartz's books, *Your Soul's Plan* and *Your Soul's Gift*, was conducted over the phone. We never met any of our clients in the books. And, to this day, when I do a Soul Plan Reading for a client, it is always over the phone or Skype —never in person—because primarily I do many hours of deep trance work ahead of time to pull down relevant past life information. Also, while I am channeling your Higher Self—your Soul—the less distraction that I have with someone around me, the better.

Now, am I telling you to call a bunch of 900 numbers and assume you are getting a good psychic reading? Not at all. You need to do your homework on all of those as well. There are some networks that legitimate intuitives, like me, are happy to be a part of, such as Best Psychic Directory. In fact, that's where you can often find me when I am not on the road. But be as thoughtful about choosing a phone psychic as you would be on choosing one in person. Check for references and testimonials. Make sure they have a "paper trail," if you will, on the internet. See if you can chat with a couple of their clients to see how they work. If, after taking those measures, you really do want to work with the psychic medium in London, Ontario and you live in Washington D.C., have no fear. Your spirit guides, angels, and the Akashic Librarians will make sure the right information gets to you no matter what delivery method you check off on the celestial order form!

CAN A READING
BE TOO VAGUE?

When a reader states they will deliver "detailed" answers, what does that mean? I asked several questions recently and paid for a "detailed" reading and each answer was about five to 10 short sentences in length. I guess I expected a bit more. The answers were so vague and general. For example, when I asked which past life is affecting me the most in this life, I got the answer, "I feel that in your last life you did not complete what you wanted to, in this life you are still working on this." In your opinion, is this detailed? I understand that the answers to Life aren't usually handed out, that we need to discover things for ourselves, but if a reading offers nothing that is helpful, how does one learn to find a better way to phrase questions or seek qualified psychics?

Secondly, I had a dream last night that could have been a past life experience, and this experience was traumatic. This dream could answer a lot of questions I have about myself and why I fear intimacy. Is it possible for a reader to home in on a specific past life, sort of a way to validate that my dream really was a past life experience?

— GAYLE

The questioner had several queries here:

* What constitutes a "detailed" reading?
* How do I make sure I'm getting a good one?
* Can a psychic help me understand a dream and tell me if it is, as I suspect, a past life?

Let's go right to the past life situation, as that seemed the most pressing for Gayle. A past life, even if only described in a few sentences, should give the client a definite feel for character/personality, a time period, perhaps a country, and a bit about WHY this is important to recall during this incarnation.

Here are some real client examples of a short but detailed past life identification:

* The constant conflict with your sister in this lifetime stems from a life when the two of you were brothers, and she stole your inheritance during the Franco-Prussian War.

* This soul has come in as your best friend in many lives past, but chose to incarnate as your father this time to give you extra support. He has ongoing Karma with your mother stemming from a life with her in 17th century Tibet.

* You have died or been killed several times because you chose to have children out of wedlock, including during the most recent previous life: in Chicago during the 1940s. Therefore, this time you chose to focus on a life unburdened by children of any kind.

When you as a client sit with me and ask for a session about your past lives, I will often give you a whole scenario. But past lives are my specialty, and I am not sure that my level of detail is a common thing. Can a psychic pick up on a dream and identify it as a past life? It has happened. In fact, one of my favorite client stories is about a past life reading I did that described a life during the Civil War. In that life, my client had been heavily involved in the Underground Railroad. The scene I unfolded for her during trance was the same dream she had been having for years, right down to what the building looked like and the dress she was wearing at the time. And she hadn't said a word about it to me before the reading.

Does this happen all the time? I wish it did! But it happens for me often enough that I know it's truly possible and not just an occasional fluke. Meanwhile, if you have a specific past life you are interested in, try giving the psychic just a couple of salient details (something like "I keep seeing myself in France running away from two highwaymen") and see if what they have to tell you matches up, or at least correlates well, with the information you've been given through dreamtime.

As for the detail situation, I would only tell the questioner that I myself am all about giving details because SHE is the one who needs to make decisions about her life—not me. So I would not count this reading, if this is all it was, as detail. To be fair, however, part of the problem may be that she received a written reading. Frankly, I hate reading by email to the point where I no longer bother with them; I can't get the information I'm receiving down fast enough. I far prefer either phone readings or recording the session to send you. When I speak, information flows better, and you get more of it because it doesn't have to process from the brain to hand to keyboard to computer page.

There are a lot of good intuitives out there, so don't give up. Just choose wisely. Always do research on them ahead of time, ask for references, and, again, remember that none of us will be 100 percent accurate.

CAN A READING BE TOO SPECIFIC?

I had a reading a few weeks ago. I was asking people a few days before if anyone could recommend a reader. I just came across this psychic place out of nowhere and she gave me a great reading. I felt happy with it, though she seemed incredibly specific. She told me the woman I would want to marry was a Gemini: with light hair and dark eyes, her name started with an L, she is not in the country but she will be by June when I meet her, her family comes from a law background, she likes to travel and write, that I shouldn't rush things, and there will be someone jealous of the relationship... I have talked to some people that know a lot on the subject and they have said that was WAY too specific and she was just trying to give me false hope when I needed it.

My question is how accurate is this reading? I mean I did see a lot of similarities, and she was pretty good at defining the current situation. However, after talking to people, I have some small doubts. Could she be this accurate?

— GEORGE

I couldn't really say whether or not the reader here was too specific for my client. I wasn't there, and I make it a point not to disparage other psychics. Frankly, however, I shy away from those kinds of predictions. Let me explain why: The woman may indeed come into the client's life exactly as foretold. Yet there may be ANOTHER woman—just as suitable, just as right for him—who would lead him on another, equally valid, lifepath. But now that he had focused on Miss L, by the psychic's prediction, he would probably ignore the second possible relationship, thus short-circuiting choice and free will.

My belief is that psychics can be mentors, but we must never be gurus. And while there have been true avatars on earth (think Paramahansa Yogananda, for instance), a psychic won't be one of them.

What's the difference? I explain it to clients this way: a mentor is likely someone who pushes your "learning envelope" a bit further than you think you can go. They push you out of the "comfort nest" a bit before you think you're ready, and encourage you to fly on your own. And they will cheer you on as you become as good (or better!) in the same field. In other words, they believe in your ability to govern your own life and have a high level of skill. A false "guru," on the other hand, often has all-or-nothing rules to follow, and encourages you to believe that THEY, and they alone, have all your answers. Sooner or later, they are discovered to be ordinary folks with feet of clay, and are rapidly toppled from their pedestals.

We can help you choose by showing you options, but nothing is written in stone. Even the order in which you do your errands can shape a future. For instance, if you go to the grocery store before the pharmacy, you could be hit by a truck. Reversing the order of the errands means the truck and you are nowhere near each other—and you live.

I have many testimonials that tell me how accurate I am, and that things happened in the order in which I talked about them during a reading. I'm always pleased to hear that, but I deliberately don't focus on my "percentage of accuracy" because then I'm concentrating on me, my ego, and my statistics. And my work is not about my ego at all. I am not important. What's important is *you* as my client. All I ever do is ask that God/Spirit/Source and your spirit guides give me the information that you need, so I can lay it out for you. As a result, I am generally very good at telling you about Life's pathways, twists and turns—but I don't name every rock, tree, and bug you'll pass on your journey!

All that said, there are some people who make a practice out of predicting this way and they can be accurate. But I certainly would not choose to allow a perfect stranger to blueprint my life in that manner.

ENLIGHTENMENT IS FOUND IN QUESTIONS NOT ANSWERS

Can you tell me what my soul's plan was for this life? What lessons am I to learn? What is my higher purpose, my mission, and how do I do it?

— CAROLINE

People come to intuitives for answers—about their love lives, their finances, their children, their parents, their futures. And often about the Huge Questions of Life, the Universe and Everything. At the same time, the majority of my clients don't know how to ask the right questions.

Let me explain why some questions aren't appropriate and why some questions lose their value if a psychic were to answer them, regardless of what the answer might be.

When I receive questions like the ones above (and these constitute a fair percentage of the questions I'm asked), I know we're starting on the wrong track. While it's valid to want to learn about such things in order to complete life challenges, these questions are too all-encompassing, and not something an intuitive ought to tackle. Why? Because figuring out our soul's plan/lessons/mission is part of our life's journey. And to ask an intuitive "what's the plan" as if the intuitive could explain the entire thing in an hour is neither feasible nor useful. Would you be able to tell me everything about your life since birth—in detail—in 60 minutes?

Even if I could do a multi-hour session without exhausting myself (or you!), I would be doing a disservice to you to dispense this monumental and vast cache of information without giving you the chance to explore, learn on your own, or piece things together. And that dismisses the entire reason you set yourself these challenges in your pre-birth planning session. We come down to Earth deliberately forgetting our unity and our complete plan in order to recreate/reconstruct it through our experiences. That's what's valuable. That's the precious treasure we bring back Home when we transition after a life filled with learning, understanding and sharing.

If you can trace a clear pattern of behavior or occurrences and want to know why the pattern repeats, how to stop it, or how it serves you—and those questions key us into an important challenge—then that's valid to review. Such information can lead to vast improvements in the quality of your life and your road to Self. But merely asking "What am I to learn? What is my plan?" is like expecting your professor to let you look at the answers before you go into your exam. How much would you really learn? And how much would you treasure those answers so easily gotten?

Let's look at some appropriate questions for a session that seeks to unblock challenges. You'll note sometimes it's a very succinct query, and sometimes it takes a little detail to flesh out, but they are always about a single focus:

* Am I supposed to write a book? Why do I constantly feel like I am supposed to do something related to writing?

* Why do I seem to constantly diminish my creative talents in favor of more commercial activities? How can I stay true to my vision yet survive financially?

* Alcohol has always played a role in my life (first father's addiction, then taken on by me at the time of his death). What looks like a character weakness on my part, can it actually be serving a higher purpose?

* Recently I have become interested in Energy Medicine courses and am wondering if it's the right direction for me in terms of added education that can improve my ability to help those I work

with as well as my own spiritual growth and physical healing. I have a deep soul urging to learn things to help myself and my clients, but I want to make sure I'm taking the course that best fits with my purpose in this lifetime.

* There is an ongoing issue with my husband and me. Sexual energy has not been there—and never was—and for some reason, this has become an issue for me since I've gotten older. I've suppressed this for years and have been looking at it over the last few years in relation to my health and as part of my spiritual development. I know you can't tell me to leave or to stay. But if you could help me to understand what purpose is being served by this relationship, that would be helpful to me.

In these questions, each client has identified a stumbling block that appears to have some duration. So, looking at how to clear the block moves their life energy forward—not only in the challenge they pinpoint, but also in many tangential areas of their lives. In other situations, they might note a pattern of desire: service through healing, the inspirational life, or the need to create something beautiful, purposeful, or enlightening.

Remember, too, that to address every single challenge in your life (near-death experiences, a traumatic relationship with your mother, a challenging love relationship, why you can't have children, etc.)

would overwhelm both of us. All of these occur-rences can spark deep questions deserving suffi-cient time for investigation and settling the ener-gies of the answer within your own emotional and spiritual purview. To expect to get and incorporate a mountain of important and emotionally charged answers from one session is asking for failure—and a heck of a headache.

So, how do you ask the right Major Life questions?

FIRST: Take some time for self-examination in order to form the questions. Do you have a re-peating pattern, a stumbling block, something that always trips you up no matter what you do around it?

Is there a part of your life that means a great deal to you (career, relationships, security) that you need to improve in a deep manner?

SECOND: Note how long the need for an-swers has been with you. Has it been building gradually, or was it triggered by a person, event, or internal epiphany?

THIRD: Make sure you are completely ready to hear whatever the intuitive has to say re-garding the answer. As always, they may not tell you what you *want* to hear ("Yes, you were meant to be a great ballerina."), but what you *need* to hear ("Movement is vital for you, but more in terms of Tai Chi or yoga than performance art.").

The determining of one's life path and incarna-tional mission is central to our flowering as a path-way to joy, service and completion. But in this case, the journey is the most important aspect of your road—not the destination. Take your time with it…

savor it…put your heart into the journey. And what you will gain is not a simple answer, but a beacon to light up all the roads here in Earthschool on which you find yourself traveling.

DANGERS AND
EXAMPLES OF
INAPPROPRIATE
QUESTIONS

When I go to a psychic, I want really detailed answers about what is going on in my life, but they never seem to give me enough. My last psychic wouldn't answer these questions, was she being unfair?

I need to know the terms of the new contract for the new loan with ___ and ___ plus details of god's [sic] plan for them to make up for botching the ___ deal and what they need to do to rectify this, plus what can they be doing at the store to make it more successful.

What is upsetting ___ and what needs to be done to have her stay at our store and when does this have to be resolved by?

What has ___ offered to entice her away from the store and what future plans does ___ have to sabotage ___ and ___'s business at the store?

I need to know if the Archangel still wants the income tax department notified of fraudulent activity by ___ and what information should be given and will I incur any displeasure from God or is this part of his plan.

Will I win the lottery and how will that affect my future plans with this current house and the business and moving out of the country?

Should I go to ___? Why should I go? Should I go with my husband? When should I go to the location/address of the property I am to buy and what am I meant to do there?

What does the Archangel want me to know about ___ and should we stay with her in ___?

Will ___ lose the store because she has lost God's favor and what has she done to cause this to happen and if so what can she do to regain God's favor?

I've intentionally omitted the name of the individual who sent this. But I'll be honest with you: when a client asks questions like this, they have crossed the line between using psychic advice and abrogating responsibility for their own life.

FIRST: Questions such as "will I win the lottery" are absolutely not the sort of question that an angel—or any true spirit guide—will answer. They are concerned with guiding you to live a good life, full of learning and accomplishments. Winning the lottery has nothing to do with anything but money. It does not strengthen you. It does not give you wisdom. It does not move you along your journey's Path, and *those* are the kinds of things with which our Upstairs Helpers wish to assist us.

SECOND: Questions asking for minute details, such as your relationship with the tax department or the precise ins and outs of a business contract with an adversary, are worldly questions. Upstairs Helpers do not particularly care one way or the other, to be honest. They are here for our soul's journey, not our personality's. Answers to such things can be determined by simple analysis, recognizing and owning what you want to do, what appears to be best in a given situation, and working toward that goal. And while the intuitive might be able to shed some light on possible outcomes through a more predictive method—such as Tarot—they will be POSSIBLE outcomes, not absolutes. If you constantly allow your actions to be dictated by what someone else tells you to do, you are not using your free will. If you make some mistakes, well, that is what we are here to do. We are not perfect. Mistakes and so-called "failures" are rerouted opportunities, neither more nor less.

THIRD: Questions like "will such and such happen because so and so has lost God's favor" are impossible to answer because we cannot lose God's favor. God is not like our third-grade best friend who likes us on Tuesday and turns her back on us on Thursday because we did something or other. That is casting God in human guise, and is a complete negation of what God stands for and God's unconditional love.

As for the rest, if you are spending so much time writing down all these questions and then waiting for a psychic—or a spirit guide speaking through the psychic—to give the answers when you should be consulting your own knowledge and responsibility, then you are wasting your time and money.

To any client, I say that if you come away from this discussion with one piece of information fixed in your mind, make it this: YOU are the one who can heal your own life, meet your own challenges, and create your own Karma. No one else. Nor, Karmically, do you have the right to insist on getting information on what other people are thinking, what they mean to do or what you are supposed to do to or about them through me. Remember what I said about remote spying earlier?

You are only in charge of your own life. And, by extension, the psychic who tells you all the myriad details you are asking for is assuming your free will is theirs for the taking. It is only a short step from asking "what do I do" about every move to a psychic saying, "if you do not do such-and-such (and pay me a lot of extra money to do it for you) then your life will be cursed."

When a client reaches this level of need, while I wish them well, I will no longer read for them because I do not think they fully understand how to work with a psychic in order to empower them-selves. Rather, they are purely focused on getting a lot of directions so that they won't "make a mistake." And that makes me, instead of a mentor, a guru in charge of someone else's life. That's most definitely not what I am—nor do I wish to be in that situation for anyone.

IS IT EVER
APPROPRIATE TO
ASK ABOUT DEATHS
IN THE FUTURE?

Recently I attended an expo in London, Ontario. The first day I was there, I had a reading done by a psychic from Ontario. My former medium had retired and I always asked her about "family gatherings." It was understood that family gatherings were funerals, but I was never told who, what, where or when—just that there would be none, one, two, etc. within the next two years, and not necessarily family. This Ontario psychic, however, was very specific about my mother and mother-in-law.

When I returned the next day to have a reading with you, I mentioned this and you were

> *upset; it apparently circumvents the legalities of the expos and local laws. My question is: I can understand this in a public expo but in a private reading can I be told, if I ask, about "family gatherings" in general?*
>
> — DEBBIE

The situation detailed above is one of the trickiest areas of psychic reading that I can think of. I will tell you right off that there are psychics who absolutely believe if they see your death, they MUST give you the details whether you want them or not, especially if it's in a possible accident situation. I am *not* one of them; seeing people's future demises isn't part of my toolbox.

First and foremost: yes, in some places it is literally illegal to predict a death, even indirectly. Philadelphia, Pennsylvania has a 60-year-old ordinance saying it is illegal to "tell fortunes, predict a death or offer to cure a curse for money." A couple of summers ago, someone in the Philadelphia Police Department dug up this dusty and outdated law and within a few days there was a sweep of every reader, metaphysical teacher and New Age store in the city. The offenders were told that if they were caught doing business after the warning they received that day, they'd be thrown in jail. Every one of them. Yes, that was a bigoted, threatening show of force by the police squad "just because they could do it" and the law (or at least the upholding of it) was overturned by the courts a few days later. But the threat is still on the books, and it's not the only place where intuitives can be harassed and arrested for little or no reason.

So that's the legal question. But what about places where it's not technically against the law? Is it proper practice? There are differing views on it, but I'll give you mine—and, yes, it's a very strong opinion.

When we plan our lives in our pre-birth planning session, we plan on several different "exit strategies." Our Higher Self sets things up so that we have multiple exit points from which to choose during our sojourn on Earth. As an example, one person's life may have four possible exits built in: dying at six from an uncontrolled high fever, dying at 27 from a car accident, dying at 43 from falling out a window, or dying at 78 from prostate cancer.

Note that there is no guarantee that any one of these exit points is inevitable (except for the last one, if the Higher Self has determined that a 78-year lifespan is "enough" for this incarnation). But thoughts are things. If a psychic (especially one you trust) tells you that they see your mother dying, if you're like most people, you'll dwell on it. If your mother gets sick, or has an accident, you will literally be waiting for her to die, because that's one someone "saw." And if your mother finds out what the psychic "saw" (and no matter how careful you are, someone is likely to spill the beans) that can drastically change her own outlook on her recovery, on how everyone treats her, on her decisions about her medical protocol—it affects everything, right down the line. And it might be enough to send your mom out of that exit door when it didn't really have to happen.

At the beginning of my full-time career, a psychic at a show I did in Liverpool, NY sat with a man who had had half his jaw removed from cancer. His wife sat with him because he could no longer speak. The psychic threw down some cards, looked at them, looked at the man's wife and callously said: "Seven months. That's all you have." How horrible! It took me, my mediumship teacher and the promoter of the fair a full evening to do "damage control."

Same thing with disease reports. A week before my wedding, I was introduced to a high-profile, well-known psychic who is on the same "show circuit" as I am. He shook my hand and immediately intoned, "Ohhh… stomach cancer, within two years, and you'll have a terrible time getting rid of it."

That was a double-barreled mistake: it put in my mind a disease I'd never contemplated having. It came from someone who has an international reputation and has read celebrities—the whole bit. And it was the last thing I needed to hear seven days before one of the most important events of my life!

It took me some work to clear that energy, even with my being a psychic, who knows all about change-your-thoughts-change-your-destiny.

What about people who don't know how to deal with such frightening predictions? Doom-and-gloom prophecies, dreadful curses—they all work the same way. If you believe them, if you let them get under your skin, you've done all the work for the one who said such things to you, and disaster almost always results.

Now, this person said that they would only want to know about deaths in general, not specific ones. Ask yourself honestly: What payoff do you get for even asking such a question and walking around with such knowledge? I would tell you only this: there is no true need to know. We all will die. Eventually, every one of your family members will be the star of a "family gathering." Use every day wisely. Make sure that every time you spend time with someone you love, everything gets said, so that there are no regrets. Get wills written, funerals planned, vacations taken, pictures snapped—LIVE! Live like tomorrow is your personal "family gathering day." And when transitions come, as they will, it will be at the perfect time. You may grieve for and miss those who have gone on, but you won't have wasted a single moment anticipating the event.

HOW TO HANDLE
NEGATIVE
PREDICTIONS

I have a personal history inundated with possible psychic predictions that came true out of my own powers. I'm curious about what you do as a psychic when you predict future events for either your own future or events in the world that you wouldn't want—from a personal preference—to happen? Not all psychic predictions are merely expressions of personal wishes or dreams. If you believe in your own powers based on your predictions coming true in the past, and you predict negative happenings that may go against something you'd want to happen, then how do you go on? How do you take any action in the world or get involved in activities that you may want to but feel very strongly won't happen by simply having faith in your own supersensitive psychic feelings-power?

— MACY

I make it a point not to assume my predictions are set in stone and absolute. Doing so surmises that there is nothing anyone can do to change a potentially negative situation. My entire philosophy of life comes down to this: "Here are your opportunities and here's how to run with them. Here are your challenges and here's how to get through them or around them." And while I believe in my own abilities, I still hold to my "even the best psychics aren't 100 percent accurate" rule.

I always make sure that the person I'm reading for knows they have free will in any situation—from failing tests to car crashes. As someone who has faced breast cancer three times, I know that the best way to deal with any tough situation or negative happening is to (a) viscerally "get" the lesson involved, (b) have NO self-pity, and (c) always ask "what's next?"

If this person is saying they have "a personal history inundated with possible psychic predictions that came true out of my own powers," then they're in trouble. It's better and wiser to completely give up the idea that they are "your" powers and accept that you are just the metaphysical garden hose through which information comes for those who seek your help. You will feel far less responsible for their actions—and you'll be more open to various possibilities on how to handle what you see in the future.

Reading over a thousand people a year, I had to learn that lesson fast, or I would have collapsed. Ego—whether it comes with pride or concern around being "right" enough for people—will short-circuit your abilities and you won't be nearly as open to potentials.

And finally, remember: what you may feel is "negative" may be precisely the event, the wake-up call, the catalyst that can catapult someone from an ordinary life to an extraordinary one. Who would Theodore Roosevelt have become had he been without childhood ailments to conquer? In my own life, had I not experienced the challenging childhood and young adult life I did, would I have been moved to do the work I have chosen, with compassion and understanding? Probably not. So even what looks to be a negative prediction on the surface may be a clarion call for something greater ahead, once the initial challenge is met.

Part Three:

WHAT TO WATCH OUT FOR

There are certain instances that are absolute red flags for me regarding how a truly professional intuitive should behave. This section details situations that you have a right to put an immediate STOP to if they happen to you. In those cases, don't worry about being polite; it's all about staying safe within your own boundaries.

DRIVE-BY PSYCHIC
SHOOTINGS

What do you do when a psychic comes up to you and insists that they have to tell you something, or otherwise gives you a reading or makes a prediction and you didn't ask for it?

A psychic walked up to me at a psychic expo saying she could tell I was worried about my daughter and something terrible was going on with her that I needed to know about. I was startled and upset, and frankly I didn't want to hear that—my wife was having serious surgery in a week and I was focused on her. (The psychic insisted that the problem was with my child, not just a vague "a woman in your life" thing.) And it turned out nothing unusual was going on with my daughter anyway, so it was extra worry for nothing. How do you keep people from doing that?

— Jerry

To be blunt, this fellow's question hit one of my hot buttons—I call this a "drive-by psychic shooting." Some psychics do feel that, when they get an intuitive message for a stranger, it has to get through. Most have the courtesy to ask, "May I tell you something?" or say, "I have a message for you," and wait for permission to continue.

A psychic who insists they have a reading for you and you MUST listen to them or something dire will happen (sometimes even grabbing you by the arm or otherwise stopping you) is trampling on your free will and invading your personal space— inappropriately, inconsiderately, and unprofessionally so. It happens to many of us.

Anyone can feel pole-axed when this happens. It comes out of the blue; you are unprepared, and those fearful and negative thoughts can take root right away unless you stop them in their tracks. The appropriate response is to interrupt the message-giver mid-sentence and say, "EXCUSE ME, but I did not ask for a reading and I do not want to hear what you have to say." If they keep pushing, raise your voice if you have to and say, "I did not ask for a reading and I refuse your information." And walk away. If they follow, you are being stalked and harassed, and should handle it the same way you would in any harassment situation: find someone in charge, report the person, and leave it for the authorities to handle.

I view reading people "across the table" in the same fashion. Psychic abilities are still misunderstood in a lot of places, and people are scared that we might be reading their minds as they walk by. A psychic who leans across his booth and says, "your dead grandfather has a message for you," or "there's a dangerous accident you can avoid; let me tell you about it" is trying to hook your emotions as if you were a fish. Their intent is to reel you and your money into their booth, short-circuiting your opportunity to find a psychic that feels right to YOU. This is not only frowned upon by legitimate psychics and show promoters, but is evidence of poor ethics on the part of that psychic. DON'T FALL FOR IT!

It's the reason why I refuse to intuitively focus on people outside my own "office," whatever the occasion or venue (private party, expo, etc.). How would you feel if your wife said hello to her OB/GYN at a cocktail party, and the next thing you knew he was lifting her skirt and discussing a diagnosis? Pretty darned upset, because (A) it's not an appropriate venue and (B) she didn't ask him to!

Having your privacy and free will honored is paramount if you are to trust what I tell you in an intuitive session. And that goes for every single psychic you ever work with. If they consider their will more important than yours, and cross your comfort boundaries—leave!

HOW TO HANDLE
AN OFF-MESSAGE
PSYCHIC READING

What do you say to a psychic who, during a reading, gets "off message?" By that I mean the psychic, instead of giving information from Spirit, launches into "Well that happened to my sister (friend, cousin, etc.) and this is what she did..." How do you get from Dear Abby advice back to the message from Spirit?

— RENEE

It's so tempting for all of us who are intuitive counselors to counsel from experience. But that's Ego talking: the assumption that our lives are important enough to affect yours. One of the things I strive to do is to be a clear channel for those I counsel. I do my best to keep personal suggestions out of the reading. After all, you didn't come and pay good money to hear about my life—you want to hear about yours!

You'll hear me speak relentlessly about keeping ego out of the reading because, if the psychic can't do that, it could be that they can't get out from under their own story. Additionally, if the psychic is at all nervous about their own reading skills or accuracy, they may immediately jump to an advisory capacity.

There are exceptions. For instance, when someone who has cancer comes to me, or asks about a relative with the disease, I tell them that I've done the Cancer Dance three times myself, and offer to share what I found useful. Then I go on and read for them to get Spirit's take on things. Any information I have for them from personal experience is *in addition* to, not *instead* of.

If the client comes to me with a career question, my years of experience as an executive recruiter may come into play; as I read the cards, there may be certain ways of handling the information that I can suggest because I counseled people in careers for years. But it's still the cards that have command of the reading. (And in the spirit of full disclosure, I tell the client that I have such experience, and ask if they would like to have me include it in the interpretation or if they would like a strictly psychic take on matters. I have yet to find someone who doesn't want to use that left-brain expertise of mine in work situations.)

Sometimes the person for whom I'm reading doesn't understand clearly what Spirit is trying to tell them. When they say, "I don't understand" or "that doesn't make sense" I might share an example in my life or another's which resonates. But that's a last resort.

It is completely polite for you to interrupt the psychic and say "Madame Hoohah, I'm sure it's an interesting story. But I'm not here to find out what others did. I'm here to find out what I should do, and I'd like to have instruction from Spirit." And if the psychic takes offense or pushes to continue the way they see fit, then you may politely excuse yourself and leave. If it's within the first five to 10 minutes of a reading (depending on how long the reading is), you might even ask for your money back, explaining, "I don't think we're connecting here."

Please understand that it can go the other way as well: an ethical psychic will know when they are not connecting with you. If they ask, "Is this making sense to you?" or "Do you understand this information?" and you continually can't respond in the affirmative, then they will feel it best to simply state that the connection isn't being made, return your money, and part cordially. In cases like that, trust that it's merely one more way the psychic has your best interests at heart.

Part Four:
WORKING WITH ANGELS AND SPIRIT GUIDES

Angels and spirit guides are an important part of the Metaphysical and Spiritual pantheon, and we all have them. None of us is smart or powerful enough to get along without them, and they dearly love partnering with us. This section shares how to get to know them and work with them.

WHAT EXACTLY ARE ANGELS AND SPIRIT GUIDES?

I'm very confused. People say that their angels are guides for them. But then other people say it's not angels, it's their dead relatives or some wizard-looking guy or an alien. They can't all be right, can they? And do they always stay with us or do they just come and go?

— PETER

When I talk about spirit guides, I talk about those discarnate beings that help us move along on our Earthwalk with compassion, wisdom, and, often, advice. But there is a big difference, for me, between spirit guides and angels—and people can often mix them up. Here is the formula:

ALL angels are spirit guides.
NOT ALL spirit guides are angels.

Our guardian angels are with us from birth to death; they do not change. But spirit guides are like our teachers. We don't have the same ones from kindergarten through our Ph.D. courses because our needs change in terms of learning, complexity of lessons, and life direction. So, too, do our spirit guides change as we grow, mature and understand our lives from a spiritual perspective. They can appear to us in many guises: human, animal, angelic, "ET," other (elf/faery/elemental), or even energy signatures.

In my own life, the original spirit guides who came in when my abilities broke open in 1994 were gentlemen with whom I was very close two incarnations ago. We were pilots together, had trusted each other with our lives in a very dangerous war, and it made sense that those I trusted then would help me through a tough "beginner's learning curve" this time.

These spirit guides have, if you will, stepped aside now. They remain as friends and I still have contact with them on a comforting level, but my main teacher now is my personal angel. My late father is also a spirit guide of sorts when it comes to my assisting folks with medical challenges: Dad was a terrific and incisive internist/cardiologist beloved by all his patients, so he's actually having a good time sticking with his former profession. My newest spirit guide was a respected Arapaho chief in the late nineteenth century.

Now, how did I know I really "had" these people? Generally, they give me information I could not have myself. At the time of his contacting me, I knew virtually nothing about the Arapaho people and their history. Everything this spirit guide told me about himself was on target and verifiable, as were the reasons he chose to come to me at that time. My father uses medical terminology that I would not know, and asks questions through me of my clients that I would not know to ask. So, in these cases, I trust that a true connection is being made between these compassionate beings and me.

Conversely, for these same reasons, I would caution you if you believe you are getting someone like Princess Diana or Whitney Houston or Robin Williams as a spirit guide. These figures are too well known, too much in people's consciousnesses now, and—in a great sense—too much in people's fantasy lives for you to be able to trust what you are getting. As a rule of thumb, if the spirit guide says it was a famous person who is contemporary in any way, or someone you're a "fan" of—living or dead—I would say it is highly unlikely that they are contacting you.

There are some very specific things, however, that a spirit guide or angel WILL NOT do. If you hear these kinds of things from that little voice in your head, put it on the Do Not Use shelf, because it's NOT a spirit guide or an angel:

* it chastises you in a sharp or mean fashion, "putting you down"

* it pumps up your ego at the expense of someone else

* it tries to "guilt" you into doing something

* it encourages you to do something that is illegal, immoral, harmful or against your highest good — something your gut knows is wrong or not in your best interests.

If you get anything like that, it's your ego talking to you, and not anyone outside you. Ignore it!

Lastly, remember that they are not necessarily here to help you with small decisions – whether to purchase the blue car or the red car, or to date Melanie or Olivia. Your angels and spirit guides are here to help you navigate your time on Earth to your best advantage – but you are still the one who determines your road.

If you want to get some concrete training on how to connect with your personal spirit guides, I highly recommend *Opening to Channel* by Sanaya Roman and Duane Packer. It's the book I used when I was first learning, and it's a great grounding source. Check our *Wingfolks* section for more information on this and other books I recommend keeping on your shelf.

And always keep a journal of your communications. Not only will it be a learning tool, but also a treasure trove of your spiritual growth in years to come.

CAN ANGELS
REALLY PERFORM
MIRACLES?

My friend said that she saw an angel make a car swerve away from her so she wasn't hit. And I've read things about people that help you and, then, when you look back they aren't there. Are these really angels? Why do they bother helping us? Seems like they'd have better things to do than direct traffic and stuff.

— JUSTIN

I'll tell you, there are more angels in New Age and spiritual marketplaces than can possibly dance on the head of a pin. Have you noticed? You've got angels on coffee cups, journals, magic wands, T-shirts, door chimes, car decals, and pet tags. Angels are the first point, for many of us, in which we cross over from an "all of this is claptrap" school of thought to "I guess there *is* something to all this Stuff." I never considered myself an angel person when I started on the Lightworker's path. To be frank, I didn't want to be. Angels seemed too Barbie-dolls-with-wings; I valued practical—even as an intuitive. I gravitated more toward numerology, with its formulae and rules. I dove into Tarot cards, whose archetypal information I found to be something concrete. Angelic beings and angel energy called to me NOT at all. Even in the beginning, when I was putting my hands on anything that looked at all metaphysical, I'd find too many angel books came across as fluffy or specious—or both.

It's rare for a person to set foot on the Light Road and *not* run into angels sooner or later—myself included. That's because angels are one of Spirit's fastest and most profound methods for dealing with dangerous situations, doubting Thomases or lost lambs. They give us signs that can't be ignored—spirit guides with definite wings. And I've experienced angel encounters that convinced me beyond a shadow of a doubt they were with me.

The first encounters happened in 1994. Suddenly, and with no training, I found myself able to do hands-on healing and talk to dead people. I couldn't explain why I could do what I did; I just knew I was being "handed my draft notice" and called to service. So, I bowed my head and used my hands. Every time I started doing my work, someone—or something—put hands gently over mine, and we worked together. People would feel presences they could not explain, and get healings neither of us could logically justify. And the presence didn't feel like any spirit guide I was aware of—the ones I heard and knew of would tell me simply: "The healings are larger than we are. Trust that."

So, I tentatively and grudgingly accepted that, somehow, I'd come to angelic notice. But I didn't want to get all "glurpy purple," as I'd tell my friends. I still wanted to be solidly based. Besides, who was I to expect angelic attention or, even more, assistance? I was neither saintly nor especially devout at that point. They had better things to do, I was sure. But Spirit certainly loves showing Its skeptics that It means what It says about love and protection.

In February of 2002, I was on a rural road in upstate New York. It had been warm, then cold, and rain had changed to a light snow overnight. Suddenly, my tires hit a patch of black ice under snow. My car swerved toward a stand of trees. I wrenched the wheel too hard. That sent me spinning in the other direction, clipping a pine tree and knocking down a telephone pole. I felt the car do a rollover, and found myself hanging, upside down, with electrical wires over the car.

I wasn't even wearing a seatbelt.

Looking back, I realize that my angels had the wheel from the first skid. They had to have done so, because at no time did I fear what was happening. It felt like slow motion, very clear. I had absolutely no fear of injury or death; it was as if I knew it wasn't my time and I was being taken care of.

I eased myself out of the car. Within half an hour, I had flagged someone down and they called an ambulance. As soon as they arrived, I was strapped to a backboard as if I'd broken every bone in my body, though I protested I was fine. I remember the EMT checking my pulse and blood pressure and saying: "You're the cool one. 120/80 and a slow and regular pulse."

I had a couple of small bruises on my shoulders. My back had been wrenched and I was in pain for a few days. But for a woman in a flipped car with no seat belt? Nothing short of miraculous. Especially when I saw my car at the tow truck's garage. It was smashed to bits everywhere except for where I had been sitting—as if there was a protective shell in that one place. Undeniable gifts of Spirit. Inexplicable, loving hands had been there in every single occurrence. How could I possibly doubt the presence of angels anymore? I couldn't. And that day, I stopped trying…

It's been years since that last encounter. My intuitive work has blossomed into a full-time career. I read for clients all over the world, and whether I'm doing divination work, channeling, healing, retrieving past lives or doing intuitive counseling, I'm still as practical as I know how to be while working with them.

But, I'm finding, there is nothing more practical than an angel when God wants to get a point across. And when I'm in a stuck place, either in my own life or while working with a client, I hold out my hand and wait for that warm touch and the rustle of a wing in my ear. It never fails to arrive in some form or another. And the assistance is as practical as I need it to be.

WHEN SPIRIT GUIDES GO SILENT

I've had a number of what I call "minor miracles" occur in my lifetime that have made me wonder about what or who is communicating with me. Ultimately, when I receive these messages I just give a wink and say thanks. For the most part, I don't really know they are messages until after the connection between the message and the reality is made. And usually, it's just a thought that "floats" across my mind. No images or voices.

I interpret this kind of stuff as my angels reminding me that they are around. I haven't noticed anything for the past six months, so does that mean my angels believe I don't need to rely on them as much presently? (Sure feels like I need them in a big way right now.) I'm curious to know your interpretation of this kind of stuff.

— PANDORA

When this extraordinary information comes through, it could well be your angels or spirit guides; but it could also be your Higher Self (some people say Soul) making you more aware of the energy connections available to all of us. Think of it this way: EVERYONE has the capability to do the kind of divination and psychic work I do. We're all "wired" like houses built from the same construction plan. What's the difference between those who get messages and those who don't? I call it the "circuit breaker" (made up of your belief systems, your cultural conditioning, and your honest desire to access that kind of Knowing). The more open you are, the more the circuit breaker is set to "off" so the power—the Knowing—flows.

The wiring and circuit-breaker in all of us means everyone can benefit from taking basic psychic awareness classes. The incarnational configuration of wiring you have may determine how you receive things. For example, I have a colleague who is very good at getting names and numbers in her mediumship. My abilities tend more toward pictures, feelings and physical structure of those who have passed. Most of the time, if you truly desire to access a precise kind of information, you can "stretch" and work your configuration so that access is available to you.

As for the question about not getting anything for six months, it could be that there are other things (stress, work, a different life-focus) that are putting connections on the back burner. Could be you are doing so well on your own that you don't need the Upstairs nudge. Or it could be that your ability to access this is so good now that you don't even re-alize when it happens! Whatever the reason, relax and enjoy the flow—knowing you will get the in-formation you need by whatever method your per-sonal spirit guides and angels deem most efficient.

DO SPIRIT GUIDES EVER ABANDON US?

> *A psychic at a psychic fair recently told me that my spirit guides were not present because they were confused as to how they could help me and thus I had been "abandoned" until they can figure out how to guide me. I found this rather odd as my own beliefs, as well as the many books I have read (including YOUR SOUL'S PLAN), reinforce that the spirit guide or guides are always present. In her reading, I felt this psychic provided a great deal of accurate information about me without asking any questions, but I found her observation odd. Can you shed light on the presence of spirit guides?*
>
> — KAREN

Spirit guides are one of the most blessed and important parts of our incarnational toolbox. In my understanding, gained from almost 40 years of metaphysical work—as well as discussing the subject with other metaphysicians I honor and trust—we all agree on one thing: Your spirit guides are always there. They never go AWOL.

This is not to say that they will continually have answers for you via divination sessions. Sometimes, because they know that growth and spiritual understanding is the #1 goal for any incarnation, they will sit things out and not give us any specific guidance. Why? Sometimes the most valuable part of a life lesson is figuring out *how* to get the answer we seek, rather than the answer itself.

However, our spirit guides are ALWAYS there on the sidelines: loving us, cheering us on, and giving us strength and courage. To know the difference between using them for guidance or as crutches— that's the trick. And there are times when all of us depend on them a little too much—more than is good for us (notice Corbie's little corvid wing raised here; she's not been exempt from that bit of learning!). That's when our spirit guides go silent, waiting for us to access our own Inner Knowing. They know we have our own answers in there; we just need to do a little digging to unearth them.

My own take on this incident is not that the client's spirit guides "could not figure out how to guide [her]." They likely saw several different and valid paths available at that Life crossroad. Rather than limit her choices, they wanted her to move forward and discover what was most important to her at this time. "Abandonment" and "confusion" are limiting, human concepts. Spirit guides (whether angels, ETs, discarnates, energy beings, or any other entity that might want to be part of your Upstairs Team) are anything BUT human or limited. Even those discarnate-but-once-incarnate human souls who are spirit guides for us have a larger viewpoint, once the body is shed.

So, with respect, I disagree with the conclusion of this psychic-fair psychic. I think she was correct in that the client's spirit guides may not have had answers at that time and, therefore, she was unable to receive anything. When such things happen with my clients, I ask them to please trust—please *know*—that those celestial seats *are* filled, as always, and the Upstairs Phone Line *is* still connected. But the call, at this time, simply is not appropriate.

And, whether or not you hear from them, your spirit guides are always sending you courage, strength, resilience and humor—because they want you to walk your Path with joy. They wish for you an open mind, open hands, and an open heart that can all help you grasp your Life Lessons and mine them for the riches they contain.

Part Five:
WHAT TO EXPECT WITH MEDIUMSHIP

Mediumship is one of the most well-known yet misunderstood talents in the Spiritual and Metaphysical realms. This section will give you some of the ins and outs of mediumship, explain the different kinds of mediumship you may encounter, and assist you in understanding what you will gain from a mediumistic experience.

THE DIFFERENCE BETWEEN MEDIUMSHIP AND CHANNELING

What is the difference between being a medium and being a channel? I get them mixed up.

— JOSIE

Mediumship, for me, has a specific meaning: someone who is the go-between, the "middleman," for those of us in form who wish to speak to our discarnate loved ones or ancestors. Some people call it "speaking with the dead," but that's rather misleading. Why? Dead supposes that there is a cessation of existence. If that were true, then it would be impossible to speak with Aunt Rose or our brother Sidney once they've left this earthly plane. And I can assure you, those loved ones I contact on the Other Side for my clients are absolutely alive!

I also see a difference between mediumship and channeling. A key part of mediumship is providing evidence of the continuity of a loved one. In channeling, the information tends to be more philosophical. Abraham, Seth, and Archangel Michael—among others—have been channeled. We have to be more trusting of the channel when there is not a historical record to which they speak.

Mediumship can be done in a variety of ways. Most people are familiar with the medium who stands in front of an audience and gets "hits" or messages from discarnate folks, and then finds the person to whom the message belongs.

Because I work with people in a timed session—and I want to get right to the soul to whom they wish to speak—I ask for certain pieces of information that do not tell me anything about the person, but will get me into their energy immediately: name, relationship, age at death, and year they crossed over. From there, I get specific impressions that allow for swift acknowledgment and recognition. It could be how they died, or well-known habits they had, or key phrases that are significant between the client and the deceased. I can get "directly heard" messages, though they also can come through in visible ways. I have found that certain physical signals can also give me information. How? If my hand thumps hard on my chest, for instance, it could mean a cardiac incident. Miming smoking a cigarette is often a key that the spirit with whom we're connecting was a smoker. My body will mimic their stance or fidgety habits. Does every medium do this? I don't believe so. It's simply the way Spirit chooses to manifest through ME. I will often also get a manner of speaking (accent, verbiage, slang) that connects me to the deceased visitor.

Once my client is assured that we have Aunt Mable "on the Spirit phone," then a true conversation can be had as I allow the Deceased to speak directly through me.

One reminder, which goes along with the no-intuitive-is-100-percent rule: When a soul crosses over, there is much to do; they're not sitting on a cloud in a nightgown with a harp. The soul to whom you want to speak may be working on their own reincarnation plans, or helping other souls, or doing other wonderful things that Discarnates get to do once they shed the earthly form. For whatever reason they choose, they may not always "be by the phone." So, when that happens, don't think of the medium as doing a bad job. Accept that the Deceased may simply be unavailable at this time—and, as the phone recording message says, "please try again later."

Channeling is the method whereby a person in form (you, me, your neighbor, could be anybody) literally "channels" information from a discarnate being (something NOT in a three-dimensional body) from another realm. Whereas mediumship specifically refers to channeling messages from those who were in a human incarnation, a channel can bring forward all manner of beings: higher life forms, ETs, spirit beings, elementals, avatars, angels and more.

Channeling is not necessarily going to send the channeler into a deep trance, though that is often the popular idea. For example, channeling can also be done through automatic writing or conscious channeling (where the channel is completely aware of and can interact with current surroundings).

Why do people channel? To bring forth information that is out of the ordinary, that is useful and compassionate counseling, or to enlighten those on their journey of Spiritual Awakening. Most people are aware of Edgar Cayce, who was a trance channel who brought forth amazing medical and spiritual information. Some of the more famous channels of today are Ronna Herman (Archangel Michael), Summer Bacon (Dr. John Peebles), Shepard Hoodwin (Michael the causal entity), Pat Roedegast (Emmanuel), and Esther Hicks (Abraham).

However, there are some beliefs about this method of communication that are way off base. For instance, the idea that a channeler is an empty vessel through which the entity comes couldn't be farther from the truth. Spirit uses everything It knows about a person volunteering to be the Bridge between spirit and humanity, and often tailors its communication to be in the best vibratory harmony. It's also a misconception that a "trance channel" (one who is not conscious while channeling is occurring) is better than one who is fully present. Which is better: a printed book or an audiobook? Neither; they both bring information forward. It is the situation that makes one more useful than another at any given time. A printed book is great on a beach vacation, while an audiobook is far more practical for long-distance driving. Either way, you take in the book's storyline.

IS THERE ONLY ONE WAY FOR A MEDIUM TO WORK?

How do you tell if a medium is doing things right? Are there certain methods, and do they all have to follow the same rules? How do I know the person knows what they're doing?

— RANDY

I often tell people I am the esoteric equivalent of a "general practitioner." A GP is a physician trained to deal holistically with the range of problems a person might have. That means they have to be familiar with a lot of different physical situations, and able to find solutions for a patient's problems with any number of different tools at their disposal.

I'm the same way. I read with Tarot and other divination decks. I can use runes and numerology. I help you connect with your spirit guides and angels. And I am a specialist with past lives. I also connect you with those who have Crossed Over, and I do that as a medium. But that simple word can raise an awful lot of questions!

Too many times people either (a) assume that everyone who claims to be a psychic is a medium or (b) don't know what a medium is at all. This chapter will zero in on the specific talents and abilities that belong in the mediumship category.

Mediumship has one overriding, primary goal: to provide evidence, without doubt, of existence of life after "death." The definition of death here merely means "when the life force is released from a physical body, and the Spirit, or Soul, is loosed from such a limiting container." As we explained in the last chapter, life definitely continues when the physical body is shed. This is the core idea of Spiritualism: direct communication with the so-called "Dead."

With that understanding, a medium is—first and foremost—a bridge between two worlds. Such a person can both send information and receive it from Spirit—being one who can, if you will, walk on both sides of the dimensional boundary, separating the "here and now" of the material world, and the world where Spirit resides.

Can anyone become a medium? Of course; I will always tell you that you can do what I do! But mediumship is an exacting and difficult calling, and therefore a truly quality and professional medium never stops learning, refining their clarity, and remaining humble in the face of what they are asked to do.

Mediumship is not cut-and-dried because our clients aren't either! Every reading is different. They are based on the personalities of the client receiving the reading, the medium giving the reading, and the Spirit or entities with whom they are working. Just as every spirit is unique and different, so are the readings and the experiences. For a medium steeped in their calling, it never gets old. The possibility of bringing exciting and important insights or messages is treasured.

A truly quality medium will be more exacting than the client, regarding the compatibility and identity of the Spirit coming forward. The medium needs to ensure that energy is compatible among all parties involved in the communication. Details, descriptions, and other solid identifiable clues will give proof of identity. Only then can the medium and the entity go on to advise or guide the client.

Mediumship is not "Madame Hoohah and her Crystal Ball," either – forget what you have seen in most movies or read in most books! There are actually several types of mediumship, which can be divided into three major areas: Mental Mediumship, Physical Mediumship and Spiritual Healing.

Mental Mediumship is what most people are familiar with. Clairvoyance, Clairaudience, and Clairsentience all fall under this heading. *Clair*, the constant in all three words, means, "Clear."

Let's give a couple of examples.

When I can see in my mind the person or guide that my client wants to connect with, that's called "Subjective Clairvoyance." I can describe in detail to the client what I am seeing. But if I actually see something in the room—whether it is a shimmer of energy or a classic ghostly presence—then that's known as "Objective Clairvoyance." I tell them exactly what is in front of me (or us).

Clairaudience is "clear hearing" the way Clairvoyance is "clear seeing." There are times when I actually hear the words that the deceased party wants to get across to my client, and such "subjective Clairaudience" is then given to the client. In my case, because of my skill with dialects and character voices from theatre training, I can often precisely give the vocal characteristics of the one in Spirit trying to reach the person sitting with me.

Clairsentience is the clear sensing or feeling of Spirit energy. This type of sensing utilizes the solar plexus of the medium's body. (That's why such sensing is often called a "gut feeling," and you have probably used it yourself more than once!) If you sit with me and you watch my contacts on the other side playing "Spiritual charades" (getting my hands or body to move to give certain clues as to what is being communicated), that's Clairsentience.

Physical Mediumship embraces Transfiguration, Materialization, and Trance. The first two are rare, and take a high degree of experience, control and clarity on the part of the medium. Transfiguration and Materialization both use ectoplasm, which is energy obtained from the Medium, other sitters, and Spirit from the world of Spirit. Ectoplasm is a substance taken from the medium's body and, according to British Spiritualist Arthur Findlay, mixed with an etheric substance.

Trance Mediumship depends on the circumstances that the medium is under at the time of the trance. It is sometimes conscious (that is, the medium is completely aware of what is going on), and sometimes the consciousness of the medium is "sent to the back of the room," if you will, and they will have no conscious memory of what occurred when they awake.

Spiritual Healing is sometimes called Hands-On Healing, and is when a medium specifically channels healing energy from the Spirit realm to the client, which again requires the medium to raise their vibration significantly.

Because being a medium is a difficult and very specialized talent, it's long been accepted that self-discipline and self-mastery are core to the necessary training. Having the gift of mediumship does not make you an inevitable Saint. But, if you decide that mediumship is a talent to which you want to devote your life, it is a never-ending quest to sharpen your talents, open your mind and heart, and dedicate your Soul as much as is (humanly) possible. Mediumship isn't simply a talent; it's a calling.

Now we come to the Séance: if you've seen the movie *Ghost*, you've seen a Séance depicted on-screen. Séances are held in a dark or darkened room. The attendees form a Spirit Circle, either at a table or simply in chairs, with the medium as the central focus and leader. At a Séance, the medium can use the energy of everyone within the Circle to assist them in contacting the Spirit world.

In a Séance, Spirit can come through in various ways. A voice can be heard from the middle of the room; it can appear to come from the Ectoplasm from the medium; or, in rare cases, a Séance Trumpet (literally a specially constructed cone made of aluminum) can magnify the sound.

I've attempted to cover all of the traditional mediumship methods and tools in this chapter, however briefly. But it is vital to understand that using these tools is a choice, and not all mediums will use all of them.

That leads me to a last but most important reminder: You should not compare mediums any more than you should compare psychics. Just because a medium uses tools unique to them rather than what has been described above doesn't mean they are a fake. There are, for instance, wonderful mediums who are artists, and receive information from Spirit that they share with their clients through Spirit portraits. I've had one of these done by a well-known Lily Dale Medium and, sure enough, there in the middle of the artwork was my father—with all the humor and droll commentary that was his hallmark. Mediums work with Spirit by offering every tool at their disposal that Spirit finds useful, and Spirit will take advantage of every energy possible to reach those Earthside with whom they want to communicate.

What I've presented here is only the very tip of the iceberg. Spiritualism and mediumship are real, viable, and a central part of life for thousands of people worldwide.

WHAT ARE THE
RULES ABOUT
TALKING TO
DEAD PEOPLE?

I was interested in talking to someone who has passed away who is important to me. I tried a medium in Sacramento, but she would not verify any information on the individual so I can know it is real. She even said the individual was with us at that time, so I did not set up an appointment with her. What type of medium are you, and can you have clear vivid conversations with the astral/celestial spirits you are talking to?

— Daniel

The first thing you need to know about ANY psychic medium is that none of us act at whim as a "Dial-a-Dead" telephone. There are occasions and situations where the departed spirit simply isn't around to talk to. Remember that we don't stop "doing" when we die because there's a lot to do outside the body. We have lessons to learn, places to go, jobs to do.

As I've stated previously, my mediumship style is specific from the get-go. I do not fish for names or relationships; I feel that is a waste of time. I seek the specific person with whom you want to communicate, using a couple of objective identifiers from you. While I ensure that you give me no leading specifics, that does get me into their energy field. I will then tell you the kind of person I'm picking up. If it feels to you as if we are getting your loved one, then I will ask the spirit we connect with for three or four things that will have meaning for you. It could be a gesture, a habit, a physical recognition symbol. It varies.

Things I have gotten:

* One father-in-law showed up with a pool cue—he'd taught my client how to play pool.

* One man showed up for my client, his son, in a tuxedo with a big red bow tie—the tie had been a family joke, and was given to the son posthumously.

* One man came in and immediately "saluted" my client, his daughter. Unbeknownst to me, she was in the Royal Canadian Mounted Police.

* One woman showed up for her former partner, and insisted that I say a uniquely personal phrase to my client, which I would have NEVER used myself (it was less than polite!)—it turned out to be the deceased person's customary greeting when she had been away.

At the same time, I would caution you against coming in with a specific set of criteria or keys you MUST receive to believe it's your person. That sets it up to be a "prove it to me" parlor game, and is never successful. Example: my father's tagline, whenever he called the youngest generation on the phone, was always "This...is the Mysterious Stranger!" in his deep and stentorian voice. And though I've spoken to him dozens of times since his death through my own abilities, and those of others, he has never come in with that most beloved and amusing of phrases. Lots of other things were on target—but never that.

Unlike the movie *Beetlejuice,* no one gets a copy of *Handbook for the Recently Deceased* upon passing over! That means there are no hard-and-fast rules about what to expect from your Dearly Departed folks. If, even without that hoped-for name or phrase, there are other valid details, mannerisms described or significant pieces of information transmitted during the session, trust that. We've connected the call.

One last caveat, at least when working with me: if you don't remember your person—say they died when you were two or, in some cases, before you were born—it's probably not going to be satisfactory for you because you won't have any visceral or "gut" memories to draw on. I'm very picky about information regarding dead people because it's too easy to get bamboozled. So, I insist on having information that you can recall from personal experience.

To find a good medium, ask to see the medium's testimonials or for references to call. If someone's truly good, the "word on the street" will let you know.

WHY WON'T MY DECEASED LOVED ONES TALK TO ME?

I went to a medium recently to talk to my mother and father, both of whom have passed. This was a medium with a good reputation, but she couldn't connect with them at all. She even told me that she wouldn't take my money and couldn't read me. She was polite and everything, but I couldn't help feeling that something was wrong with me. Why won't my parents talk to me when other people get their people on the Other Side? I feel them in the house so I know they are around. I am sad and confused.

— Betsy Anne

This is a question that is often asked with grief and bewilderment. What could the client have done that their loved ones have turned their backs? That's when, with complete compassion, I reassure my client that it's NOT THEM. Sometimes those on the Other Side don't come through and it's nobody's fault. It doesn't mean they don't love you. And it doesn't necessarily mean that the medium isn't good (especially if they've done readings for other people who were able to report that the medium made contact with the Other Side). It simply means the connection wasn't there at the time.

Here's a good analogy:

You sit down at a computer. It's a good computer, and you are a good computer operator. You want to get on the internet, but it just isn't happening! Now, does that mean you are NOT a good computer operator? No, it doesn't. You know how these things work. You are competent, and that has not changed. Does it mean the computer isn't any good? Not necessarily; if every other function is working, all the wiring is sound, and it's plugged in—then it's not the computer. IT'S THE CONNECTION TO THE INTERNET THAT IS OFF-LINE.

With mediumship, the idea is essentially the same. The connection, for whatever reason, may not always be there on any given day. Remember that our loved ones don't "sit by the heavenly phone" waiting for it to ring, or for a chance to talk to you. They are doing marvelous things on the Other Side: resting, learning, expanding, perhaps being spirit guides for other folks on the Earth plane, or helping to shepherd souls that are making the Crossing (I had one client whose father, a decorated veteran of World War II, made it his business to help soldiers who were killed in the Middle Eastern conflicts to make their transition peacefully and without fear). It's also possible your loved one could be planning their next incarnation.

If you have felt them around you in your house, then you know that they still love you and are deliberately sending you that knowledge and comfort. But just as our Earthbound friends can be out doing things when we call, our loved ones can be just as happily busy Upstairs. Leave a message on their answering machine by sending them love, perhaps spending a few minutes in prayer wishing them well. They will always get THAT message.

And Finally:
CAN I DO
THIS TOO?

Over and over, for all of my career, my clients have heard me tell them: "I'm not special. You can do what I do." In this section, you'll understand why.

IS DIVINATION JUST FOR EXPERT PSYCHICS?

I'm interested in learning about divination, but a friend told me that it takes years of practice and that other psychics won't like me "horning in on their space." Are either of these true?

— SOLANGE

Divination has long been viewed as the province of specially gifted persons, such as prophets, shamans, and magicians. If that's your view of Divination, you should not consult an intuitive counselor. Period!

In general, people fear knowing the future, yet are almost desperate to do so. Prophecy has been a pivotal part of countless plays, stories and morality tales, to the point where a simple crystal ball or deck of Tarot cards can engender terror in those who think they have no control over their own lives if the instrument of divination tells them disaster awaits.

The truth is this: Divination can work to show you the hidden significance of events, offer suggestions for avoiding life's pitfalls, and give you some ideas of what the future may hold. But YOU, Dear Reader, are the one who determines how you will take and use that information.

As I said in the very first chapter, there are literally hundreds of ways to look at the future and the past. Today, divination is used to give you tools to predict likely options and make your life what you want it to be. If I have a sign above my desk on the Astral Plane, it reads, "Here are your opportunities and how to grab them...here are your challenges and how to get through or around them...here is YOUR toolbox, go rock and roll!"

In this section, I'm going to discuss methods of divination that I use myself, along with some views of those intuitive methods that are specialties of some of my most trusted colleagues. There are four general criteria regarding divination methods that you need to understand before consulting them or someone who uses them:

FIRST: Always remember the "Rule of 85%" that I've mentioned throughout this book. You will not be perfect in your readings, and that's part of the learning curve.

SECOND: If you are human—with a reasonably functioning brain and open to trial-and-error and practice—you can learn to get the information flowing through your psychic channels. However, it takes actively wanting to do it; it's not an autonomic function like breathing.

THIRD: You are in charge of your own life. What you discover through the process of learning to read is information—not a directive from the Universe that you will collapse if you don't follow the message to the letter.

FOURTH: There is nothing evil in what we do. Not a thing. All of the tools and information gained through their use are NEUTRAL, the way a fire is neutral: it can either warm a house or burn it down. But what is DONE with the fire determines its value. Religions that view this work as Satanic, evil or sinful are religions that generally do not want people to seek answers outside what the Authorities tell them they should know. Spirit guides and mediumship differ from divination by what they resent, how they work and what they reveal. (Parts Four and Five of this book are devoted exclusively to what they do and how they work).

THE BASICS FOR STARTING DOWN THE PSYCHIC YELLOW BRICK ROAD

I. Ground...Center...Shield. It is vital that you know how to ground, center and shield. It's the same as if you were going out hunting, scuba diving or flying an airplane. Until you learned basic safety, were absolutely clear on the technical parts of the equipment, and had many, many hours of practice and training, you wouldn't be considered safe!

What is *Grounding*? It's just what it sounds like. Think about what it means outside the metaphysical realm when someone says, "that person is really grounded." It means they are steady, stable, and present. For a novice Lightworker, being grounded is all that and more.

A standard exercise is either sitting (feet on the ground, arms and legs crossed), or standing with feet slightly apart and finding your balance. Then, imagine roots growing out of your feet, diving deep down to the center of the earth. Know that Gaia (Mother Earth) is welcoming your roots, helping you stabilize yourself and accepting any negative energy within you that you'd like Her to transmute and clear. This connection is so important—it reminds you that you are connected to All That Is, and not walking this road alone!

Centering, the second step, is where you bring the energy that you are pulling up from the Earth and hold it in your physical center—your heart or your solar plexus, depending on where you truly "feel it." Centering is the process of being completely present in your body. It is being aware of your boundaries, your senses, your wholeness. We have our attention split dozens of ways in this multitasking world, but centering asks you to bring everything back to Home Base.

Breathing—deep, even breathing—will help you be aware of your self, your cells, your Beingness as you bring yourself back to the Central Point.

The third part of this basic exercise is *Shielding*. Shielding won't help you avoid being hit by a bus. Nor are we suggesting that there are Big Evil Things always lurking around the corner to get you. But shielding *is* about protecting yourself from distracting energies, other people's negativity, or the general miasma of the world today. If you are going into a highly charged situation (a bad neighborhood, a difficult business meeting, a court appointment, or even a holiday get-together with the family), shielding will blunt and buffer the effects of people and situations whose energy clashes with yours unless, or until, you specifically want to engage with it. The easiest form of shielding is to imagine yourself in an egg or bubble of White Light stretching at least two to three feet beyond your actual body. If you want a real-life example, think of a hamster in a hamster ball running around the living room floor safe from Muffin or Max, the bigger four-legged family pets!

II. Meditate. Every day. Meditation isn't just for those who are interested in Eastern religious practices. Meditation is an absolute necessity to keep your one-pointed focus strong and sharp.

Think of someone trying to cook: they are dealing with knives, fire under the pots, and other things that can be dangerous if their focus is distracted by a whining child, the phone constantly beeping with messages, or the pets running underfoot. In order to successfully prepare the meal, the cook may have to order everyone OUT, shut the phone off, and put the pets in another room or in the yard.

Or consider working on a large project for a chief client. The finished product is how you ultimately present yourself to your superiors, your customers, and your teammates. If you've been given a complicated assignment, or a lot is riding on the result, you'll want everyone and everything to LEAVE YOU ALONE until it is completed to your satisfaction.

Working in the spiritual and metaphysical realm will have you connecting with and encountering events, energies and beings that you have not met before. In order to understand them, stay safe, and interact with them successfully, you will need to have a mind that cannot be easily or quickly distracted. Mishandling energies or leaving your shielding down because you're distracted can be as dangerous as confidentiality breached, or the too-long sleeve brushing by the open flame. One unguarded moment, and you're in trouble.

There are also positive aspects of meditation as well as protection. When you learn to shut down the constant "squirrels in the brain"—the carping voices and nagging reminders—you'll feel calmer. You'll find yourself able to think more objectively. You will actually feel stronger, restored, and replenished—ready to deal with the everyday world as well as those interesting events that happen during your spiritual explorations.

Meditation doesn't necessarily mean sitting on a zafu cushion staring at the wall, however. There are many ways of going about the exercise: something as simple as sitting quietly and concentrating on your breathing can slow the mind and bring you peace at your center.

When you notice your breathing, don't get caught up in its rhythm or the number of breaths per minute. Simply notice the breath, observe it going in and out, and feel it in your body. If you notice yourself thinking and losing focus, don't berate yourself. Just make a mental note, *Thinking*—and return to paying attention to your breath.

As little as ten minutes a day of meditation can get you started on this path of serenity and focus.

III. Keep track of your progress without judging it. There's an old saying: "One 'oh crud' erases ten 'good jobs.'" In other words, we tend to remember the dumb mistakes and botched efforts, and dismiss the on-target experiences as coincidence, or imagined. DON'T! Don't do that to yourself. That's why it's vital to keep a pad and pen (or open computer window in your Notes application) so you can keep close track of your hunches, your gut feelings, your unusual observations, your initial readings and explorations. Don't let your fear of being wrong cause you to deny a message from Spirit. Messages come in many ways and at unexpected times; if a message doesn't resemble what you read in *How to Become a Metaphysical Master in a Year and a Day*, that doesn't mean it isn't valid.

My mediumship is done in a style that I haven't seen with anyone else. But it works for me. My clients tell me that when I get their Uncle Irving, I get it right, with all the details and nuances. And they get to talk to Uncle Irving directly. I do not have the "wiring" to do mediumship the way John Holland or James Van Praagh does it. But if I thought that was the ONLY way mediumship worked, there are thousands of people who would have missed the experiences they had with me in talking to the Other Side.

Along with this, it's all right to be a little skeptical, a little picky about the information you're getting. Assuming everything you're getting is honest and correct is just as bad as assuming it's all wrong.

Trial and error happens within learning to use your extrasensory talents, too. If you find that using psychometry (reading the energy in an object) only yields correct information for you about one-third of the time, but Tarot and Oracle cards seem to fly from your hands with a far greater percentage of accuracy, then pay attention to how you're naturally wired. I'd encourage you to keep working on the psychometry (or whatever skill is tougher for you to master) because it's always good to put another skill in your bag. But don't assume you have to be as fabulous with one tool as you are with another.

And keep a journal. I'm not talking about a grown-up "Dear Diary" exercise, but a place where you can record your experimentation, your adventures on the Path, and your thoughts about your Journey. Pagans, Wiccans and Witches have Books of Shadows, and Alchemists have their Hermetica. You, too, should have a central place where you keep track of your metaphysical adventures.

CONCLUSION

I hope *The Psychic Yellow Brick Road* has answered some questions, piqued some interests, and shown you that the marvels of metaphysics are well within your reach. After reading all the parts and chapters of this book, you should now have a taste of What's Out There. As you continue on your psychic discovery, I encourage you to you walk the road wisely—keeping your eyes and hearts open—with the curiosity of a Martian detective who judges nothing and asks questions about everything with open delight!

You're welcome to sit at *my* table with me at any time.

WINGFOLKS

Think about those breathtaking V-formations of Canadian Geese that you see every spring and fall. The flocks fly hundreds of miles to get to their seasonal nesting grounds—but they can't do it without supporting each other. That's what these suggested peripherals are all about, getting wonderful support as you begin your journey of Psychic Discovery. (And if you see something mentioned here, I have read or used it and can recommend it from personal experience.)

Psychic Protection: Balance and Protection for Body, Mind and Spirit by Ted Andrews. Ted Andrews was a beloved and well-respected intuitive and shaman who wrote a plethora of volumes on metaphysical subjects before his death in 2009. His book on psychic protection is one I find very accessible for people just starting on the Metaphysical Road. It covers many subjects that "rookies" run into—including what is and what is not real in the psychic world, dispelling a lot of myths and superstitions. He then discusses the Spiritual Road, how to walk it safely, and the responsibilities therein. If you are just starting out, I recommend that you add *Psychic Protection* to your library.

Opening to Channel: How to Connect with Your Guide by **Sanaya Roman and Duane Packer.** This is the book that taught me how to channel thirty years ago, and it's as relevant today as it was then—even with its later revisions. Roman and Packer, working with their own guides Orin and DaBen, teach all the basics that are so important: what channeling is, how to prepare for it, what guides are and how to work with them, how to protect yourself from unwanted intrusions, and how to read for others. A great basic book, and one that has served me well in my professional life.

Meditation for Beginners by **Jack Kornfield.** A key name in the field of meditation, Kornfield gives step-by-step instructions on this most basic of metaphysical practices. This book is intended for folks who have never meditated or who are sure they won't be able to! You can listen to the guided meditations included in the CD or download them online. If you understand that having a daily meditation practice is vital to the rest of your Psychic Road, you will especially appreciate the tips on making it a daily practice.

Angel Chatter: Heavenly Guidance and Earthly Practice to Connect with Angels by **Christine Alexandria.** Christine has brought angelic work down from the "glurpy purple/too sweet/Hallmark" realms into real, practical and detailed working methods. Her book is filled with information, resonances and attributes for fourteen archangels that will give you a thorough grounding in Angelic Lore and how to work with these Wingfolk to bring your life into balance and perspective. Now that Doreen Virtue has stepped away from the field and no longer validates her former work, Christine is the next authentic and empowering Angel Expert to step into the spotlight, and takes up the Angelic mantle with humor, compassion and confidence.

Two Hawks Gallery (twohawksgallery.com). Two Hawks Gallery, run by David and Lee Seaward, is Central New York's largest purveyor of crystals, stones, and minerals—as well as a full range of other metaphysical items. For 27 years, Dave and Lee have searched the world for gorgeous and useful materials for those on the Psychic Road. They are careful with their selections, generous with their information, and my go-to place for the most important crystals I use for metaphysical work.

ACKNOWLEDGMENTS

ANITA MERRICK: My sister psychic, also known as Crystal Wind. The first to read the manuscript in its entirety! Thank you for your thorough review, assuring me that I did indeed avoid the flying monkeys.

BERNADETTE CARTER-KING: A dear friend and shining example of How To Run A Metaphysical Business With Integrity. So very glad you were an integral part of the book this time.

BERNI XIONG: Once more my genius editor, who smoothes my prose and crystallizes my ideas without changing my voice one iota. Couldn't do it without you, partner!

CHRISTINE ALEXANDRIA: My spirit-sister of the printed page. You understand what it takes to get a book out from start to finish, and were always encouraging, loving and sharply observant. This book is better because of your involvement.

THE MEW CREW: McKittycreek's Baron Manfred, Shubacoons' Captain Oswald, and Echidna's Leviathan (Prawn to his friends)...I completely admit, I could never write as well without a Maine Coon in my lap, or in front of the computer screen, or yodeling for MomCat to come and take a break. You keep me grounded in the best and most loving possible way.

STAN MALLOW AND RAY FAUCHER: Promoters par excellence of the First Star Psychic Fairs in Canada. For years, you have been prime examples of what true professional psychics are all about, from "both sides of the table." Much of what I have spoken of in this volume, I learned from you. Thank you for your constant encouragement and generous mentoring.

And as always...

CARLE KOPECKY, Husband First Class, who has watched me live everything I've talked about in this book—good and bad, enlightening and frustrating –and supported me throughout the process.

ABOUT THE AUTHOR

CORBIE MITLEID has been on the mystic's path for over 40 years—meeting challenges, always questioning, leading the "examined life." This road has illuminated an essential Cosmic Truth: God gives all of us what we need for a life filled with miracles and joy. As long as our hearts are open, whole, and aligned with our Source Energy, anything is possible. (And it never hurts to bring laughter on the path with you!) If Corbie can share that blessing with you, she feels she's doing things right.

Corbie is a psychic, channel and medium, and has been reading since 1973. She travels coast to coast across the United States and into Canada as a full-time intuitive counselor. Corbie has inspired and helped thousands of individuals every year as a teacher and facilitator, frequently appearing on radio and television. She is a featured channel in Robert Schwartz's breakthrough series on Karma and pre-birth planning, *Your Soul's Plan* and *Your Soul's Gift*. Corbie is also the author of *Clean Out Your LifeCloset*, the first volume in *The Self Development Project* series.

Corbie's certifications and affiliations include Certified Professional Tarot Reader (through the Tarot Certification Board of America), membership in the American Tarot Association, and ordination as a minister of the Sanctuary of the Beloved (Order of Melchizedek). Corbie's specific skills include Tarot and Oracle/Divination card readings, spiritual/intuitive counseling, past life retrieval and analysis, mediumship, and spirit guide conferences (including speaking with one's Soul or Higher Self).

For spiritual resources, articles, and events calendars, or to schedule a private session with Corbie, visit *https://corbiemitleid.com*.

For information or to check out the resources we've mentioned in the book, visit: *https://thepsychicyellowbrickroad.com*.

To leave an honest review and star rating, go to the book's listing on Amazon.com.

Also by Corbie Mitleid...

TAKE CHARGE OF YOUR LIFE – LOVE YOUR JOURNEY!

CLEAN OUT YOUR LIFECLOSET encourages you to write your own story of change based on your history, your life experiences, and your personal goals.

Through stories, examples, and just-for-you-designed "Adventure Pages," you can find your own answers, design your own toolbox, and discover that healing the old and creating the new can be positive, joyful and soul-satisfying.

"Funny, straightforward and non-preachy... Mitleid does not intimidate or taunt readers with unattainable goals. Rather, her book is an approachable, supportive, and unassuming manual in achieving self-actualization through growth and spiritual exploration. An inspiring work that sets itself apart from other self-help books."
— KIRKUS REVIEWS

Named one of the IndieReader Best Reviewed Books for October 2017 by Huffington Post: *"With smart ideas, presented in an elegant and customizable way, CLEAN OUT YOUR LIFECLOSET may just be the compassionate, endearingly quirky companion self-help readers are looking for."*

ISBN: 9781614683704

Available in paperback, Kindle and Audiobook at
AMAZON.COM *or* SHOPTBMBOOKS.COM

Along with being a psychic medium, I'm an inspirational speaker and facilitator. When you are in charge of your changes, all possibilities are yours as well – which is the basis of my first book, *CLEAN OUT YOUR LIFECLOSET*. In the following excerpt, we explain about The Self-Development Project and share with you how to find clarity in your life via the *Joy of a Clear Telescope.*

CLEAN OUT YOUR LIFECLOSET

THE SELF-DEVELOPMENT PROJECT

CORBIE MITLEID

About The Self-Development Project

The Self-Development Project and its peripherals have been structured to support your "inner Martian" by encouraging you to use what you read in the way that suits your needs best. I'll make suggestions, but they are just that—a suggested road to self-study. If there is any other underlying purpose, it's to teach you how to play again without worrying about The Rules, right or wrong answers, or matching up your findings with anyone else's.

The Self-Development Project is all about how you Can't Get It Wrong. By picking up this book and reading this far, you've already shown up for Day One of The Life You Want class. You are standing right here with me. You have everything you need to make the changes you seek, to embrace the things you want to keep, and to have a ridiculously good time—without checking to see if it's all right with the Professor (that's me).

You get an A for showing up. Simple as that. Because showing up means you will have picked up what you needed to learn to go out in the world and figure out your own answers to the exam—which will always be the right ones.

The Self-Development Project is a series of three books: *Volume I: Clean Out Your LifeCloset, Volume II: The Big Reboot,* and *Volume III: Be Your Own Masterpiece.* This handy little trilogy will partner with you in totally turning your life inside out and upside down until you've got an entirely self-created life.

Think of this series as the literary equivalent of that big mural of paper. We encourage you to draw the Ultimate You with a huge box of crayons, a batch of finger paints, glue and scissors, and sparkly bits—whatever takes your fancy!

What You'll Learn in Volume I: Clean Out Your LifeCloset

This first installment of *The Self-Development Project* consists of a total of sixteen chapters organized into four sections as follows:

Part I: Getting Clear.

If you are standing in the middle of a maelstrom (think teenager's bedroom), you have to get clear on what is currently in disarray. Focusing your telescope is how you set yourself up for that clarity. You'll take a closer look at places in your life that are like a three-legged stool—if any one of them is wobbly, you fall down. *Getting Clear On Your Purpose* helps you figure out what you're doing here. *Getting Clear In Your Relationships* helps you get the most out of your interactions with people around you. *Getting Clear With Spirit* helps you keep all the parts of your life in perspective.

Part II:
Simplicity and
Living Well With Less.

As you're cleaning up that proverbial bedroom, you will have detritus to clear out and duplicates to toss—some of the belongings may even be unrecognizable underneath all the dust and grime. It's the same way with life. I'll encourage you to look at life as a Tiny House—the idea that you have core essentials worth keeping, allowing everything else to be up for discussion. You'll find out how happy you can be with what you have, not what you *think* you *need*. You'll discover the delicious value of experiences rather than "Stuff." And you'll put on your practical thinking cap deciding which items to keep or toss out to simplify your existence.

Part III:
Going With the Flow,
Learning To Adapt.

Going with the flow is one of the easiest ways to open up your life. We're going to turn the idea of perfection on its ear. You'll learn why perfection isn't what you think it is, and that you have more of it than you realize. You'll find out that stumbling toward enlightenment is valuable. You'll examine those times when perfect destroys good. And because exceptions prove the rule, you'll discover when it's perfect to stand your ground or when saying "No" is a fabulous idea.

Part IV:
Stress Is a Complicated Friend.

This section covers that inevitable in-your-face companion of 21st-century humans. Not all stress is inevitably bad. We'll talk about the difference between good stress and bad stress. You'll learn how to listen to its messages: recognizing when stress is a warning sign, when it's like a hot water tap you can shut off with a little nudge, or when it's that freight train of "Are you kidding me?!" barreling down the tracks and needing your immediate attention.

The Adventure Pages.

You'll notice that at the end of each chapter, there are Adventure Pages. These pages are where my book becomes *our* book—yours and mine. You'll answer some questions to help you reflect on what you've read. You'll come up with places in your life where these ideas will work. You'll get to decide what your personal takeaways are (we call that "putting arrows in your quiver"). And you have space to write down what you believe to be the Most Important Piece of Knowledge you've gained. We'll encourage your inner artist to create a picture of what you've learned from every chapter along the way—making *Clean Out Your LifeCloset* into your own personal divination deck.

Playing with the Adventure Pages will enable you to see how my ideas can work for you. They highlight the parts of your life where you want deep change. They allow you to find your own way of phrasing things. And, I hope, they coax your Little Kid side to come out and play.

Part I:
Getting Clear

The Joy of a Clear Telescope

From the massive Keck structures on Hawaii's Mauna Kea to the simple ones that dot backyards on cloudless nights, telescopes transform hazy vistas into brilliant clarity. Viewing a distant star can activate wonder, a desire for adventure, and a profound sense of the vastness of the universe. But no matter what such breathtaking vistas trigger, our newfound clarity changes our worldview.

Like those stars powdering the skies, our lives are full of dreams, projects, plans, and ambitions. We can work on prioritizing our heart's desires. We can figure out how to give ourselves enough time to do them. We can let go of other people's dreams for us that have nothing to do with who we really are. Most importantly, we can decide what is essential for us in the long run.

Once we've acknowledged the goals and dreams we want in our life, we may still be left with a hazy mass of possibilities.

How do you pick a focus? Must you choose one dream out of many? Can your different goals support one another, or do you have one overriding desire?

How do you bring the thing you want most in the world into dazzling clarity?

Let's look at some helpful tips to keep your internal telescope sharp and focused.

Decide To Use Your Telescope

Your first step is to decide that gaining clarity is a priority. As Ralph Blum wisely says in *The Book of Runes*, "...even more than we are doers, we are deciders. And once the decision is clear, the doing becomes effortless."

The decision to seek clarity is, in itself, an action that will bring forward motion and excitement to the process of getting clear.

Clean the Lens

No matter how beautiful the view is outside, you'll never see it through a dirty window. That's why we have spring cleaning, to scrub away the winter gunge that's built up during those months of hibernating. A little spring cleaning of our internal telescope can get the glass sparkling and the vista sharp and enticing.

But what happens when the lens of your internal telescope continues to film over with daily diversions? Such deflections can be many and varied—and they take away from what's important. You may feel pressure from the urgent things that clamor for immediate attention: *Do the laundry! Run the errands! Play with the cat!* You can be seduced by the mindless things that are easy distractions: internet surfing, television, video games, and texting. You might feel emotionally entangled with someone else's situation, pulling you away from your own state of affairs.

All of these detours get in the way of accomplishing what truly matters to you: writing that article, planning a family night, exercising, meditating. When you look at all of the time-wasters and distractions, you'll come to realize you can set them aside—but that will require you to focus your telescope.

Focus Your Telescope

The world today provides us with more information than we can possibly process. If we fail to set limits or boundaries on where we focus our attention, we fall into a numb, drifting mind-state—never knowing where to rest and always feeling overwhelmed. Rather than settling for mindlessness, seek mindfulness.

Mindfulness is magic. When we are mindful, we pay attention to our life. The present moment is very much alive, yet we look at what is going on—both in and around us—without an emotional charge. Being mindful means we are actively making choices about our precious time and mind-space. When we use mindfulness to focus, clarity is the result. With clarity, you can "aim your arrow true." You will be able to identify a distraction quickly and find it easier to set it aside. You will catch yourself when you're thinking self-defeating thoughts and bring yourself back to productive mind-talk.

Pay attention to those times you find yourself thinking, *I can't do this.* Notice when you habitually berate yourself, compare yourself to others, or bemoan your current circumstances. These destructive thoughts and self-beliefs are the film and dirt on your internal telescope lens.

When you notice such self-talk, it's time to change perspective. Choose to think differently. Compassionately remind yourself of what you want. Is it possible for you to get it, do it, or make it happen? Yes, yes and yes! Be gentle with yourself as you go through these changes. Your mind is like a puppy; whapping it on the nose with a newspaper will not get you the outcome you want. You'll need time, repetition, and discipline to create a new habit with this mindfulness. Think of it as leash training your puppy, with treats at the end!

Aim Your Telescope

Meditation will keep your internal telescope from wobbling on its base. Too many people think meditation means sitting on a zafu cushion for hours at a time striving for no-mind. Think of meditation more as a calming of the chatter. Find time— as little as ten minutes a day—to sit quietly. Let your mind go softly silent. Coax your mental squirrels off their squeaky wheels for a while.

As your mind stills, those *urgent* beasties tend to go and sit in a corner. What you want to focus on quietly comes to sit with you. When it does, you can truly examine this most important companion and its friends, so you (and they) can work together most efficiently.

Meditation brings serenity, consolidating your energy for optimal use. The calming of the mind is one of the most powerful calibration tools your internal telescope can employ. The more you practice meditation, the more easily your mind will come into alignment.

Adjust the Lens

The beneficial structure of both you and your surroundings is crucial for clarity. Your body is the housing for your telescope. If your body isn't in sound working order, then neither are you.

These are nine simple ways to adjust your internal lens.

1. Cultivate simple, good habits. Get enough sleep. Eat good food at the right time, your attention centered on the meal. Avoid haphazardly shoving food in your body while on the go. Exercise to remind your body that you are partners in this adventure, which is good for raising your endorphin level.

2. Keep yourself and your surroundings clean and comfortable. When you're neither distracted by clutter nor feeling scruffy, focus is easier to come by.

3. Get dressed every day. Working in pajamas may sound lovely, but if not getting dressed dulls your clarity and confidence, the comfort isn't worth the trade-off.

4. Turn off the techno-tempters when you need to stay focused. According to Timothy Egan, contributing writer for The New York Times, a survey of Canadian media consumption by Microsoft concluded that a person's average attention span had fallen to eight seconds—down from 12 seconds in the year 2000. We now have a shorter attention span than goldfish. Why? Because our attention span shortens the more we indulge in electronics.

5. Set your schedule and keep your lists. Sheer willpower may not be enough to keep you on track, especially if you have numerous distractions throughout the day. Following a schedule and prioritizing items on a list helps to keep you focused.

6. Learn from other people with focused telescopes. The Law of Attraction states, "where your attention goes, so goes your existence." If you want clarity, then surround yourself with people and things that will cultivate clarity—not dissipate it.

7. Stay away from people who live in Neverland. Avoid people whose lives are filled with "no," "not," and "never," who make promises but never keep them, and who are habitually late. Eschew the company of the drifters who have no direction. They exhaust your energy with unproductive talk about dreams they'll never pursue because they're unwilling to do the work.

8. Find your tribe. Your true tribe is comprised of those who are excited by life, whose direction and purpose are at the tip of their tongues, and whose lives reflect their goals and desires with promise and effort combined.

9. Avoid the gloom-and-doom in the world. The adage in broadcasting is "If it bleeds, it leads." That kind of outlook is the last thing you need around you! Make an effort to find positive stories and inspirational books and podcasts. Listen to the words and ideas of those whose clarity of purpose and spirit has brought them joy and success. If they can achieve a happier state of being as they reach for their dreams, so can you.

Now that you have your telescope cleaned, set up, and aimed at the stars, the future is a lot clearer. Whether you choose to focus on your purpose, your relationship, or your spiritual growth, it's no longer a bunch of twinkly smudges above your head. There are vast galaxies of possibility—and they're yours to discover.

The Adventure Pages:

The Joy of a
Clear Telescope

What was your personal definition of "Clarity" before you read this chapter? Any changes?

Have you been able to find Clarity on your own? How?

What ideas in this chapter went *PING!* for you?

Any idea where you'd like to aim that telescope?

Put more arrows in your quiver: What three things do you want to take from this chapter and put to use in your life *right now*?

Here's your Invention Page!

Write down those three arrows on the blank page below. Draw, collage, or otherwise illustrate what your personal "Joy of a Clear Telescope card" would look like.

....

Want to read more?

Check out the full book, available at:

AMAZON.COM *or* **SHOPTBMBOOKS.COM**

....

Rev. CORBIE MITLEID

PSYCHIC MEDIUM • CHANNEL
INSPIRATIONAL TEACHER

Corbie's mediumship and past life expertise are showcased in the international bestsellers

YOUR SOUL'S PLAN & YOUR SOUL'S GIFT.

Intuitive Counseling • Tarot Sessions
Mediumship • Spirit Guide Conferences
Past Life Retrieval and Analysis
Seminars, Lectures and Workshops
Corporate and Private Events